Keto Living Fat Fast Cookbook

A Guide to Fat Fasting For Weight Loss
Including 50 Low Carb & High Fat Recipes

TABLE OF CONTENTS

SAVORY MEALS

SWEET SURPRISE

APPENDIX I: FAT FAST RECIPES – KETO LIVING COOKBOOKS

FOREWORD

Welcome to the Keto Living Fat Fast Cookbook!

This is my 4th Keto Living book. The 1st contained a selection of Keto recipes for all meals of the day. The 2nd explored the variety of savory and delectably sweet snack options Keto has on offer and the 3rd was filled with beautiful photography showcasing the flavors of Keto.

This is a fairly unique book in the Keto Living series in that it strays from my usual cookbook-centric fare and instead also delves fairly deeply into a pretty cool area of Keto, Fat Fasting.

Done right, and safely, Fat Fasting is a really useful strategy to break through a stall in weight loss and return to a state of Nutritional Ketosis.

With the occasional Fat Fast I've personally managed to achieve some amazing results in my own weight loss journey, and because of this I wanted to share some insights into the protocol and a selection of 50 delicious recipes, perfectly suited for Fat Fasting.

In the pages ahead we'll go over the finer details of what a Fat Fast is.

After a synopsis of what a Fat Fast entails, we'll visit the origins of Low Carb dieting and Fat Fasting and take a look at relevant pioneering studies and exciting results.

I'll dig deeper into what's involved in this simple yet effective protocol and also talk about Nutritional Ketosis, why this matters, and how we can measure it.

Importantly, we'll look at safety considerations, such as who should and shouldn't embark on a Fat Fast, as well as allaying a few fears or questions you may have, and examining the smart way to approach any kind of dramatic dietary shift.

Then we'll take a few pages to examine some of the higher fat foods that make up an important part of our recipes ahead.

And after that, we'll get stuck into 50 delicious recipes designed to make the whole journey an adventure, rather than a chore. There's really no need to stare at a block of cream cheese for three days straight! Not with all the choices ahead.

In an Appendix at the end of this book, I've included a list of all of the recipes found in my first 3 recipe books that also fulfil the requirements for a Fat Fast. You'll more than double your Fat Fast recipe repertoire if you have access to these books in your library.

Without further ado, we have some really interesting ground to cover! ☺

Ella Coleman

DISCLAIMER

Before we get started, let's go over a couple of things.

Firstly, in regards to the nutritional information found at the bottom of each recipe.

I've done my best to fastidiously calculate the macro nutrient breakdown, however obviously there will be variations in the creations coming out of kitchens of all my readers due mainly to brand choices, different cuts of meats etc.

Based on this, please understand that as a general rule the nutritional information provided should be fairly close in the calculations, although is ultimately included only to serve as a beneficial guide to keeping you on track. As an FYI, Net Carb count has been calculated by deducting the dietary fiber from the total carbohydrates.

I certainly hope that the info proves useful and accurate to you, and of course if you wish to double check my calculations on any recipe, I would always recommend that you please do so if you feel the need.

In regards to the Fat Fast diet itself, although much of the information within has been researched thoroughly and is believed to be reliable, myself (the author), publisher and associated parties make no representations and in no way claim to be health care professionals, or qualified to give health care advice.

I encourage you to read the sections in this book relevant to health related cautions and safety when considering commencing a Fat Fast to ensure beforehand that the protocol is right for your particular condition or circumstances. Recipes may also not be suitable for everybody, as each person's condition, needs, allergies, prescriptions etc. are different.

As mentioned in several places throughout this book, I recommend anyone undertaking any kind of dietary change to first seek medical advice from your health care provider, or physician.

Lastly, although studies surrounding the Fat Fasting concept have been conducted for over half a century, the actual term *Fat Fast*, was originally coined by Dr. Atkins in his bestselling *New Diet Revolution*.

The author and publisher make no claims or representations to be in any way affiliated with the Atkins name or associated branding and instead intend the publication to be a study of, overview and guide to the concepts and potential benefits of the protocol, completed with a selection of recipes suitable to the criteria of the protocol.

Now that's all out of the way, let's begin!

FAT FASTING

WHAT IS A FAT FAST?

A Fat Fast is a short term technique usually used to overcome a metabolic condition during a period when your weight loss plateaus or comes to a stall.

This might happen somewhere along your journey to your goal, or even at an earlier stage of the diet, while your body is still adapting to operating smoothly on a Ketogenic diet.

The term *Fat Fast* was originally coined by well-known low carb, high fat advocate, Dr. Atkins[1], and is based on a fascinating study by British researchers in the 1950's that we will explore in the next chapter.

The goal of a Fat Fast is to force your body to start burning fat again through a process called lipolysis, a process that can give a real kick in the pants to a stall and get things moving along again in the right direction.

The basic guidelines of a Fat Fast is the consumption of no more than 1000 calories per day with 90% of those calories coming from fats, normally broken into 4-5 feedings of around 200-250 calories spread out over the course of the day. More on this later.

The protocol is performed for around 3 days, although running a Fat Fast for up to 5 days is not uncommon, and some folks like to mix up the system into their own unique flavor such as running a Fat Fast for one day at the start of every week, for example.

It's important to point out that a Fat Fast is not necessarily suitable for everyone, especially if the scale is moving as it should be. For other people, such as those on certain medications, the protocol can even be dangerous.

I'm not trying to scare you though. There is a lot of interesting science behind it all and although precautions are important, in the grand scheme of things for most *healthy* individuals, reducing calories for only a few days and increasing fats on a diet where fats are already high shouldn't be cause for too much concern.

A basic rule of thumb before you choose to begin a Fat Fast, is to make sure you **are** experiencing an actual stall before considering a Fat Fast. This will help you determine if you are experiencing insulin resistance and an associated metabolic condition.

Also, you should only attempt a Fat Fast after having attempted a Keto diet for some weeks with no noticeable adverse health effects from being on the diet.

Needless to say, undergoing any kind of dietary changes should be discussed with your doctor to ensure you have no medical considerations, and I'll go into more detail on any safety concerns, and in which situations you may need to exercise caution in the pages ahead.

Let's begin by looking at what constitutes a stall.

SLOWED OR STALLED WEIGHT LOSS

As a food enthusiast and lover of how all things work, I find it liberating to know the mechanics of what is going on behind the scenes in my body, and this knowledge has most definitely helped me stay on track with an understanding that things were happening as they should be.

There are many reasons weight loss may slow, or stall during a Ketogenic diet.

Post Induction Stall Syndrome

Early on, during the initial stage of the diet, most people lose a nice amount of weight quickly. I remember when I started on the Keto diet, I lost around 9 lbs in the first week, and immediately thought I had found a miracle cure.

This initial burst of weight loss does wonders for confidence in the Keto diet, and also gives a much needed boost to self-esteem and a glimmer of hope for a better, leaner future. Fantastic, right?

Sure, however it's important to know that the truth behind these initial losses in these days while your body is still Keto-adapting is that whilst some of the weight loss you experience will certainly *be* fat, a significant amount is also water.

You see, a gram of carbohydrate molecules inside your body stored as glycogen (a storage form of glucose), is bound with a few grams of water molecules, so... as the glycogen is used up in the absence of being replenished quickly enough, this heavy water also become waste, and is dumped as well.

Make sense?

So there you are, a short time into a brand new diet and noticeably lighter. Full of excitement from those early losses after this initial whoosh, it is **normal** at this stage for your weight loss to begin to slow.

What's happening is this. When your body adapts to the reduced carb intake, adjustments take place and some water retention is normalized. This can result in perhaps a pound or two of water returning, and during this same period you may also burn a pound or two of fat. The offset you see on the scale as this ballet takes place *appears to be a stall*, and is otherwise known as Post Induction Stall Syndrome.

This is normal, yet for many the initial rush of elation from early weight losses is replaced with disappointment from the temporary stall, and faith is lost in the entire diet.

After a quick descent into premature despair, a tub of ice-cream appears in the lap, the carbs return with every mouthful and along with this a torrent of glycogen clinging water bringing us right back where we started.

The lesson here is **don't give up!**

Please be careful in labeling the natural flow of things a stall pre-emptively. Post Induction Stall Syndrome is not a good reason to begin a Fat Fast.

Note: *Please don't reduce your water intake to try and flush water from your body. Our bodies most definitely don't work like that.* **Drinking lots of water is a good thing and actually benefits weight loss.** *I go over this in greater detail later.*

What exactly is metabolic resistance or metabolic syndrome?

Note: *If you aren't sure what is meant in the below by Nutritional Ketosis and Insulin Resistance, don't despair. I cover this and the science behind fat mobilization in an upcoming chapter, but for now just know that for most people, a state of Nutritional Ketosis is the goal on a Keto diet to maximize fat burning.*

We have established that there is an expected slowdown in weight losses after the initial water weight component has dropped, so what next? Well after this, following a standard Ketogenic diet should expect to return you results on a regular basis.

However, if you are *metabolically resistant* or have *metabolic syndrome,* your weight loss may continue to stall after this.

Metabolic resistance is a term coined by Dr. Atkins to indicate an inability to lose weight even after carbohydrate or caloric restriction.

Metabolic syndrome is a medical diagnosis and is characterized by the presence of at least three out of five key risk factors, one of which is abdominal obesity and usually accompanied by a similar trouble with losing weight.

Technically they are not the same thing. It's possible for example, to have metabolic syndrome yet still be able to lose weight. However, both are associated with insulin resistance and associated difficulty in losing weight, and can affect the ability to enter into a state of **Nutritional Ketosis**.

Regardless of which term you choose to go by, I find it ironic that a condition that makes it hard to enter Ketosis and lose weight is helped to heal by entering Ketosis and losing weight.

Metabolic syndrome is actually more common than you'd think.

At the time of print, for example, Wikipedia estimated a whopping 34% of the adult population in the USA as having some form of metabolic syndrome with obesity playing a major part, influenced by several factors including age, hormonal issues, physical activity and medication to name a few.

If you are overweight, often sedentary, and have trouble losing weight there is a reasonable argument that you may have metabolic syndrome to some extent.

Even if you are doing everything right, tracking and testing, if you are resistant to insulin and have a metabolic condition, your body will be unable to easily make the switch from burning carbohydrates to burning fats, and weight loss will be hard.

Especially in situations where the weight gain you have accumulated has come primarily from a typical high-carb Western diet, your body may need some help getting into a state of Nutritional Ketosis to facilitate a return to fat mobilization.

It's just a matter of getting the ball rolling to begin with.

Enter the Fat Fast.

A Fat Fast by its very design, severely curtails both carbohydrates **and** protein. The result is that your metabolism **has** to turn to fat, in the absence of any other option. This kick-starts a process known as lipolysis, releasing Ketones and ultimately leading to Nutritional Ketosis.

Before we commit to commencing a Fat Fast as an easy fix prematurely and start labeling ourselves as metabolically screwed, there are several other factors we need to ensure aren't happening first.

Let's go over some of the ways that we unwittingly sabotage our progress and stall ourselves.

The scale isn't moving!

Be certain of this reassuring factoid. That little scary set of digits we see when we step on to our scales is **not** indicative of your overall fat content.

The number that tells you your weight on the scale isn't telling you the exact ratio of fats, water, muscle, bones and organs– it's simply doing what it's supposed to do, and weigh **all of you**.

Perhaps you haven't stalled at all. Your body composition is very likely to be changing – consider this if the scale isn't traveling in an overall consistently positive direction every week.

There are however, technologies that **can** quantify with great accuracy your exact fat percentage, such as hydrostatic weighing, and DEXA scans (which I recommend if you have a desire for accurate tracking), or calipers, when operated by the right person.

Another method of detecting fat content found in many homes is a feature of our digital bathroom scales. Many of these scales claim to be able to accurately calculate body fat percentages through Bioelectrical Impedance Analysis, but in reality are largely flawed and inconsistent making this a fairly unreliable tool.

Finally, a good old fashioned tape measure can be one of the best low tech ways of seeing quantifiable progress. That and of course, how your clothes are fitting you!

If after some time and testing you are **certain** that some other factor is at play, let's look at our other options.

Are you restricting carbs enough?

On a Keto diet, carbs should really be restricted to less than 50 grams a day, and in the early days while Keto-adapting, under 20 grams is even more preferable. If you are eating more than this, it could easily be the reason you are stalling.

Be careful to check for hidden carb laden ingredients at home and when eating out. For example chicken wings are low in carbs, but that BBQ sauce? Blue cheese sauce may be better. Carbs can add up quickly, especially in drinks.

Also, when you do eat carbs, the **type** of carbohydrate you eat makes a big difference. High GI carbs should be avoided as they bring about the very spike in insulin we are looking to avoid.

When choosing your carbs for the day, lower GI is best. For example, fruits such as berries are a reasonable choice, and you can kind of go into unrestricted mode with many high fiber, non-starchy vegetables as it takes a lot of celery for example, to make up even a few grams of carbs. Eat your greens liberally and without guilt. And not just your greens. Tasty vegetables like mushrooms and peppers also fit the bill!

I've written more on what foods are great to stock in your kitchen in a later chapter.

Note: *On a US nutritional panel (different in other countries), fiber should be **deducted** from the carbohydrate count to get your **Net** carb count. It's the total of all the Net carbs that make up a daily carb figure.*

And alcohol?

There are high carb alcohols like beer, and low carb alcohols like spirits.

However, although alcohol chosen properly may be low in carbs, your body **prioritizes** burning alcohol before anything else, so burning of fats takes a back seat while alcohol is being removed from your system.

Drink enough, and fats will build up while your body continually processes the removal of alcohol. Also many of us know that bad diet choices slip in when inebriated.

It's easy to stall or even head in the wrong direction if you don't have a calculated plan, so make careful drink choices and exercise some moderation.

Done right, many people report being able to enjoy a couple of no-to-low-carb drinks here and there without any noticeable change in results. I myself enjoy a glass of pinot noir now and again, preferably from a New Zealand winery, so there you have it!

Are you eating too much protein and not enough fat?

Fat Fasting For Weight Loss Including 50 Low Carb & High Fat Recipes

After first eliminating a large amount of carbohydrates from our diet, we next need to look at our protein and fat consumption.

Pause for a moment. Make sure this sinks in, and **don't** just gloss over to the next section.

Are you eating **enough** fat?

If calories from fat aren't making up over 60% of your diet, then in all likelihood you aren't.

It takes time for a newbie Keto enthusiast to wrap their head around as foreign a concept as eating enough fats. It just seems counter intuitive on what is essentially, a fat loss diet.

It's true, deeper Ketosis is obtained with a higher fat percentage in your diet.

Yet our bodies need protein to survive, and protein is an excellent and necessary muscle sparing and muscle building macronutrient. Still, too much can adversely affect our ability to enter into a state of Ketosis.

It turns out protein can also elicit an insulin response, albeit nowhere as dramatically as carbohydrates. The good thing about protein is it also stimulates glucagon, an insulin countering hormone, so we aren't as concerned about metabolic impact. In excessive amounts however, it becomes a factor.

So for example, removing carbs and eating lean chicken breast all day won't provide enough fat and the quantity of protein will likely affect you reaching the state of Ketosis you are looking to achieve, especially in a resistant individual.

A basic guideline for protein is to consume around 0.8g per pound of lean body mass (total weight less fat weight) for sedentary people, and up to as much as 1.2g per pound of lean body mass for a bodybuilder.

If you **are** a bodybuilder on a Keto diet, the subject of protein intake for muscle gain really requires more detail than this, and you'll benefit from visiting the ketogains subreddit at www.reddit.com[2] where the science behind macro nutrients intake is broken down in intricate detail, to suit various exercise, cardio and bodybuilding regimes.

For those not looking for such regimented figures, just aim to keep carbs low, and fats high.

For example, a little bit of lamb, some avocado, alongside some creamy cauliflower mash sounds like a tasty and well balanced Ketogenic dish to me... Oh look, now I've gone and made myself hungry.

Are you rewarding yourself with *cheat days*?

Keto adaptation can take time, weeks in fact to make you into a fat burning furnace.

Although there may be an ongoing argument for athletes to introduce periods of carb ingestion (and there are also plenty of athletes that don't even do this), as a rule, there is no need for the rest of us to need a cheat day.

It may resonate with you to hear my story.

In my early days of Keto I fell into the trap of allowing one *cheat day* a week where I would eat a pizza with my family, maybe a chocolate ice-cream and a few carb riddled snacks through the day. Ultimately this prevented me from ever really entering a state of Nutritional Ketosis. It was only after I replaced these meals with Keto alternatives and allowed my body to become truly Ketone fuel adapted that my results picked up considerably.

In our mission to lose weight we need to fix both the chemical relationship we share with food and **also** our emotional connection.

Now I **totally** understand that in real world day to day situations (especially on the weekend), we go to a lot of places where eating carbs is hard to avoid. At cinemas, social gatherings, clubs and dinners, carbs are everywhere and it can be hard to deal with the pressure felt during these times.

Often we make questionable choices with a plan to *catch up later*.

Knowing this, and being reasonably adept in the kitchen, I set about trying to create a variety of Keto substitutes of popular foods to prove that eating Keto does not need to mean going without.

For example, my 2nd Keto Living book contains 101 recipes full of savory and sweet snacks, including everything from pizza to ice-cream.

I propose the solution is to spend time in the kitchen preparing substitutes of some of your favorite snacks.

And on your next *cheat day* simply enjoy a few extra serves of your homemade Keto goodies, stay within your carb allocation and the rewards will soon be evident. It's better to increase the calories on this day then increase the carbs.

Make sense?

Are you up to date with all the tweaks?

The more you look into the science, the more you realize that there is several tweaks you can play around with to help polish the process.

For example, a little endurance exercise throughout the week will improve glucose tolerance.

Some fat in your morning coffee is suggested to may have a metabolic benefit and useful for keeping away hunger pains.

It's worthwhile looking into **Intermittent Fasting**, another great technique to help breakthrough a stall. This protocol involves consuming no calories at all for a set number of hours each day and then consuming all your calories within a set timeframe, such as only eating between noon and 8pm every day.

Drinking a lot of water is good for many things that help the body burn fat, one of which is beta-oxidation, a process of breaking down fatty acid molecules.

And as it turns out, **glycine** may also help break a stall, helping glucagon out from the pancreas, which in turn gives the fat cells a nudge to trigger fat release and burning. Glycine can be found in several sources such as gelatine (get the sugar free flavors), pork rinds or supplemented.

More diet tweaks are coming to light all the time. It's fun to keep abreast of the little things that give us the edge, but be careful to separate actual science from a sales pitch.

What next?

If after you've put some energy into all the above possibilities you've still seen no new record lows for several weeks, you may well be stalling due to metabolic reasons such as insulin resistance and a candidate for a Fat Fast.

Stay calm. With a little bit of focus, education, some effort and time, one way or another we will find a way to accomplish our goals.

Please consider looking into the many friendly and informative Keto communities online, such as the one at www.reddit.com/r/keto[3] so that you're never far from support when you need it most.

I'm not 100% certain I have metabolic anything? I just really want to lose weight fast for a special event... Can I hurry things along with a Fat Fast?

This question is on too many lips to be ignored, so let's consider it for a moment.

A Fat Fast is designed to not only push you into a state of fat oxidizing Nutritional Ketosis, but also into a restricted caloric state for several days.

There's no denying that a Fat Fast will help you shed weight and might I add, somewhat rapidly if you have excessive water weight to lose, so if your aim is to look good for a photograph, a class reunion or a hot date, a day or two on a fast fat could help you reach your goal.

Ask yourself, how soon is the event and is there enough time to make a difference?

Do some calculations in your mind as to what kind of results you can expect to achieve.

Firstly, have you eaten a lot of carbohydrates lately? A Fat Fast will help flush out a lot of stored glycogen along with the attached water molecules which may account for a quick result.

If not, and you have essentially already been in a state of effective Nutritional Ketosis for a period of time, then the actual weight losses will be less, although you should still expect to lose some fat from the caloric deficit and level of Ketosis.

But, a warning first.

A Fat Fast diet was never meant to be abused.

In Dr. Atkins's bestselling book, *New Diet Revolution*, the protocol he suggests is not even mentioned until Chapter 20. Aiming for a quick fix and snap results is not as effective long term as the values of positive reinforcement and long term commitments to new good habits.

In actuality if you no metabolic syndrome or resistance, enter Ketosis easily and lose weight appropriately, a Fat Fast is not recommended or even considered necessary and can in fact be dangerous for some individuals when pursued.

I keep mentioning this warning, but you should be able to get a rough estimate yourself if you are in this category. Ultimately it is up to you, and your medical advisor to decide whether this applies to you.

As the author, it's my job to ensure I recommend caution in any decision towards dietary change and the questions I need to ask are to be thorough are;

Have you discussed your plan with your doctor and have his approval taking into account any current existing medical conditions that you may have?

Are you reasonably healthy and feel that you know your body well enough to attempt a Fat Fast?

Do you have a metabolic condition that's causing your weight loss to stall and have you ruled out all other possibilities for the stall?

If your answer is yes to these questions, then I can't see any good reason for you not to experiment with a few days on a Fat Fast.

For me, the Ketogenic diet and occasional Fat Fast have worked positively, and I attribute Fat Fasting as a powerful tool in having returned me to a state of Nutritional Ketosis quickly after any moments in life where I find myself having slipped with my carbohydrate intake (a definite problem when visiting family on the holidays no matter how hard I fight it!).

Personally I've Fat Fasted not only to break a stall, but also for impending social gatherings on occasion with varied levels of success from each cycle.

I endeavour to keep a good distance of time between Fat Fasts, and I usually only stay on them for 2-3 days each as I'm not as resistant as I once was and my weight goal is getting closer all the time.

In the next chapter, we will look at some of the history surrounding the Ketogenic diet, Fat Fasting and a look at some clinical studies on the protocol with astonishing results.

THE ORIGINS OF LOW CARBOHYDRATE EATING AND THE FAT FAST

Before we delve too deeply into the intricate details of a Fat Fast, we really should take a little trip down memory lane and see where it all began.

In the mid-1800s, a coffin maker and rather a stout fellow named William Banting found himself miserably obese at a time in history that obesity was not nearly as commonplace as it is today.

His ailment was of the extent that he even had to descend staircases backwards to avoid straining his poor load-bearing knees.

In an earnest effort to lose the weight, he tried every popular slimming regime of the time, including Turkish baths, purging, increasing activity and reducing what he ate, and even with the guidance of some of the most eminent physicians and scientists of the time, nothing was working.

As he eclipsed the age of 60, he eventually had packed more than 200 pounds on his 5 foot 6 inch frame.

Complaining of hearing problems, Banting visited an ear, throat and nose specialist, named Dr. William Harvey who concluded that the primary cause of the ailment with Banting's hearing stemmed from his obesity, and in his professional opinion on the matter, was the result of an intolerance to carbohydrates.

Willing to try anything by now, our Banting followed Harvey's dietary plan and sure enough, lost nearly 50 pounds in less than twelve months.

Although a fairly unrefined regime, by cutting out sugar, beer, potatoes, and almost all bread from his diet, Banting found himself largely following a high fat and protein, and low carbohydrate diet similar to the kind of eating we who live Keto all know too well!

Dr. Harvey also limited Banting to a weighed amount of food. We had no means of measuring calories then, but we know now by his well-documented eating routine that this equated to around 1200 calories per day, accelerating his fat loss even further.

In 1863, fuelled by his personal victory, he released his now well-known, somewhat controversial at the time pamphlet, *A Letter on Corpulence*[4].

His method was refined and his publication increased in popularity, and by the 4th edition his pamphlet had grown from 25 pages to over 100 pages, was full of testimonials and had sold over 50,000 copies.

"Do you Bant?" was a phrase often heard amongst the Keto pioneers of yesteryear and although doctors at the time dismissed the diet as peculiar and branded Harvey and Banting charlatans, Banting was not cowed by the medical establishment and lived slim and trim to a ripe old age of 81, no small feat in the 1800's.

Fat Fasting For Weight Loss Including 50 Low Carb & High Fat Recipes

As the years rolled on, various notable names suffering from a similarly hefty problem followed Banting's pamphlet with success, including the Earl of Salisbury, of Salisbury steak fame.

Soon after the First World War, Dr. Alfred Pennington was hired by large American chemical firm, E.I. DuPont to tackle the obesity problem of staff members.

With inspiration from Banting, a diet of low carbohydrates combined with high fats and proteins came together again to help 20 obese employees drop an average of 22 pounds each, in just 3 months.

Curiously, his patients on this restricted Ketogenic diet also appeared to be burning stored body fat rather than muscle tissue, even though caloric intake was reduced. Pennington reported that far from experiencing a drop in metabolic rate, his patients had sufficient energy in their stored body fat to actually maintain high metabolic rates.

More and more it was becoming apparent that the idea of a calorie is a calorie is a calorie was simply not telling the whole story.

Skipping ahead to 1944, a cardiologist at a New York hospital named Blake Donaldson reported successful treatment of obesity using a diet that included a minimum of 24 ounces (680g) of fatty meat each day.

Patients were encouraged to eat until they were full, and even though some of them seemed bent on exploring just how much more than that they could eat in a day, patients kept on losing weight.

Studies continued to be conducted around the world, pushing conventional dietary theory further out the window.

In 1956, in what is now known as a flagship study[5] in low fat experimentation, British researchers Prof. Alan Kekwick and Dr. Gaston L. S. Pawan, took a closer look at the findings published by Dr. Pennington surrounding calorie type in body composition.

Although it seemed fairly clear that calorie restriction in varying levels should lead to quantifiable weight loss, Kekwick and Pawan really wanted to explore the hypothesis further to determine whether the type of macro-nutrient that made up a calorie mattered, specifically in relation to weight loss.

They intended to not only document weight loss, but also to see exactly **what** was lost depending on dietary variation.

And so, an exciting and very telling scientific test was performed.

For the first part of the experiment, a group of clinically obese subjects followed a so-called *balanced* diet (a blend of all macro-nutrients), for cycles lasting between seven and nine days with the only variation being a different caloric level in each cycle, ranging between 500 calories a day up to 2000 calories a day.

From this test they discovered when patients were consuming fewer calories, they achieved more weight loss than the higher calorie phase of the experiment.

Now that in itself wasn't *especially* surprising of course, but... the second stage of the study **was very surprising**.

As a follow up, everyone in the study now ate a diet that across **all** subjects, was just a flat 1000 calories a day, **but** in each stage of the test the **types of calories** fed to the subjects varied. These diet stages included a baseline mixed or *balanced* diet; a diet that consisted of 90% carbohydrate; another with a composition of 90% protein; and lastly, a diet that contained 90% of the calories from fat.

Now... shall we guess at the results of this test?

Surely, my dear readers, (many who are already staunch Keto converts and perhaps can guess where this is heading), surely if all that is important in a mathematical weight loss equation is the *number* of calories consumed, then logic would dictate that every time this test was run, subjects would lose an equal amount of every time. Correct?

Well... as it turns out, and is often the way in this big, beautiful planet of ours, logic sometimes needs a kick in the backside to wake itself up to scientific reality.

The results of this test were it seemed, not at all what a calorie-in, calorie-out mindset appeared to dictate.

Without further ado, let's look at which feeding period **did** result in the most weight lost.

First it's important to note that even at a mere 1000 calories per day, *when the subjects were consuming the diet consisting of 90% carbohydrate they didn't lose **any noticeable weight at all**, and in actuality gained an average of 0.24 lbs per day.*

When on the *balanced*, or mixed diet, they did in fact lose some weight, although not nearly as much as when on the high-protein diet achieving an average weight loss during this phase of 0.6 lbs per day.

And lastly, to the surprise of the researching doctors, (but perhaps not to us), *the cycle that achieved the greatest weight lost was the diet of 90% fat.*

During this period, subjects lost on average, **a colossal 0.9 lbs per day**.

Critics at the time (and some today), suggest water weight played a major factor in the variations, however water balance studies done by Kekwick and Pawan showed that weight losses were definitely not all water.

In fact Kekwick and Pawan were very thorough, studying fat losses in waste, water losses, and even insensible water losses which is the water we lose minute by minute from our bodies during the day and while we sleep, indicative of metabolic advantage.

Again, the high fat diet produced the most significant results.

17

To quote from the study, "If these observations are correct, there seems to be only one reasonable explanation – namely, that the composition of the diet can alter the expenditure of calories in obese persons, increasing it when fat and protein are given, and decreasing it when carbohydrate is given…

"…It is however, surprising as regards fat, whose action in this respect seems to be even greater than that of protein."

This important study formed part of the foundation of research establishing a low-carbohydrate diet as effective for long-term weight loss.

For our needs, in continuing to chart the history of the subject of this book, we need to extrapolate forward from Kekwick and Pawan's 2nd study. The resulted weight loss from the diet consisting of 1000 calories a day and a 90% fat content were significant and directly relate to Fat Fasting, our area of interest.

The next most commonly cited study[6] in the history of a Fat Fast was from 1965, when Dr. Frederick Benoit at the Oakland Naval Hospital followed seven obese men as they were put on a total zero calorie fast for ten days, *essentially in a state of starvation*.

At the end of the fast, the men had lost an average of a whopping 21 lbs, but carried a notable downside.

Almost 14 lbs, nearly two-thirds of that weight lost, was from lean mass including muscle, and the remaining 7.5lbs from body fat. That is far from ideal.

The same men repeated the exercise, now eating 1000 calories a day and of that, 90% being fat. They continued to lose weight, but this time, of the 14.5 lbs lost, 14 lbs was body fat, **doubling the fat loss of the starvation state**, and with only 0.5 pounds of muscle mass lost.

Again, in this example water may account for some of the initial rapid weight losses, but we can see that a pattern of preserving muscle, and accelerating fat losses is starting to form, and this is really what we are looking for, a repeating pattern in this kind of test.

Another study[7] in 1971 by Charlotte Young tested for various levels of fat loss on diets of 1800 calories per day, in conjunction with 3 levels of carbohydrate intake.

There's no surprises here either – On 104 grams of carbohydrates a day the subjects lost 2 lbs of fat per week out of a total 2.73 lb weight loss. On 60 grams of carbs a day the subjects lost 2.5 lbs of fat per week from a total loss of 3 lbs, and finally, on 30 grams of carbs a day subjects lost 3.73 lbs a week with almost all of that weight loss coming from fat mass.

In 2002 a study[8] by respected author, Dr. Jeff Volek conducted at the Cleveland Clinic over 42 days, used very accurate DEXA technology to measure results that again show notable fat losses and significant muscle sparing on a 2200-2300 calorie, low-carb (46 grams a day) diet.

Side by side, these equivalent patterns speak volumes to me, and show a really strong case for low carb, and the benefits and results of Fat Fasting.

More and more studies are appearing all the time.

I admit… I like to dig around and play devil's advocate, looking for answers to questions on how results were measured. Water weight is of special interest to me, as some studies don't document every little component in detail, and I wonder to myself things perhaps not present in every conclusion.

Questions such as;

How long was there between each round of tests? Did subjects return to a *normal* diet between each round of testing? Were subjects already glycogen (and water) depleted after each study?

It's a blessing and a curse as the more I dig, the more fun I am having but also the more questions are raised, and I just end up reading more and asking more questions because I'm genuinely interested.

I also believe that when it comes to this kind of research, many books are guilty of cherry picking information for the most sensational responses, and even though a great number of scientists, doctors and advocates of Ketogenic diets may say something to be true, I feel that if I am putting my name on something, even if I'm drawing from the conclusions of lofty heavily researched papers, I need to have a darn good understanding of and confidence in what I'm writing on a comprehensive level before sending it to print.

Personally, I take comfort that the patterns from these examples show a strong correlation to each other and remain consistent in their findings in relation to the benefits of a low carbohydrate diet.

In addition to published medical journals and studies, I can attest to my own significant weight losses on a Keto diet, and also from spending time online in Keto communities such as the one on www.reddit.com/r/keto I've witnessed a veritable cornucopia of success stories, and progress pictures from those living Keto that not only confirm the scientific protocol, but warm the heart to see.

The benefits of a Fat Fast to those who need it are evident, eliciting rapid weight loss and swift elevation of Ketones. These changes help bring about a state of Nutritional Ketosis that can be maintained long after returning to a regular Ketogenic diet for an awesome fat burning response.

I encourage you to keep reading, learning, watching videos and questioning everything.

A MODERN DAY LOOK AT THE MECHANISMS BEHIND A FAT FAST

HOW DOES IT ALL WORK? EATING FAT TO LOSE WEIGHT DOESN'T MAKE SENSE!

For those new to a Ketogenic lifestyle, the Fat Fast probably sounded counterintuitive the first time you heard about it. It seems to fly directly in the face of the most widely regarded nutritional guidelines, like the USDA's Dietary Guidelines for Americans[9].

Decades of dietary theory have urged us to get about half of our calories from carbohydrates.

Yet the studies we examined in the previous chapter have shown that we should question this.

SO WHAT EXACTLY TAKES PLACE INSIDE US WHEN WE EAT CARBOHYDRATES?

Your body will burn whatever fuel it can access, with a priority to remove alcohol first, and then glucose.

After consuming carbohydrates, your body then digests and absorbs it as glucose, causing a subsequent spike in blood sugar.

This peak is followed by an increase in production of insulin by the pancreas. Insulin is a regulator of the metabolism of carbs and fats in the blood, and so when it arrives on the scene it detects the excess glucose and starts its job of pushing the blood sugar into cells.

In a nice healthy individual it only takes a little bit of insulin to bring blood sugar back down and push much of this fuel into the cells where it is most efficiently burned, such as muscle.

When an excess of blood sugar builds up from carbs faster than can be processed, insulin needs to store it away. Fat cells are the perfect place to house that excess.

Another side effect of insulin is while it's moving around doing its thing, it's inhibiting lipolysis (fat mobilization) and isn't co-operating in allowing fat to escape from fat cells.

When cells become resistant to insulin (common in people with metabolic syndrome, obese people and Type 2 diabetics), the body produces more insulin to deal with the load. And in the process, this drives more and more fat into the fat cells.

To make matters worse, if fat cells aren't releasing fats, then your body starts demanding you give it more food for fuel. You'll eat more and more and then the cycle repeats itself.

If you are insulin resistant and going through this cycle, it indicates an intolerance for carbohydrates, and following a diet that advocate high-carb, low-fat at this point only perpetuates an already negative cycle.

SO WHAT DO WE DO?

By shifting our diets to higher in fats (around 65-70% of our calories), moderate protein and under 50g a day or less of carbohydrates (better if kept under 20g during the first weeks of Keto), our body goes through some positive changes as the destructive cycle stops and the damage begins to reverse.

Less insulin is needed to regulate and push blood sugar into fat cell storage, fat becomes mobilized again, and your body starts operating on Ketones as a source of fuel.

Remember, even a so-so attempt at eating low carb can cause problems.

For example, if you eat a big, high GI potato with a fatty steak, the potato becomes the primary source of energy and the insulin it brings to the party helps to keep the steak fat stored away for later.

The effect of fats you eat is in many ways dependent on the quantity of carbs and your biological response to the carbs you eat, so stick to lower GI carbs and stay within your allocated limits.

KETONE SPEAK

Ketones – Produced by the liver from dietary fats, these little metabolites provide fuel to the cells of the rest of the body and are an alternative energy source to glucose. Ketones are measured in millimoles per litre, (millimoles per liter are abbreviated as mM).

Ketosis – This metabolic state is determined when a raised level of Ketones is present in the body.

Nutritional Ketosis – This is the measured range of Ketones in the blood stream (greater than 0.5mM, but less than 3.0mM) that we are looking to achieve for the safest and most efficient state of Ketosis to maximise turning our bodies into fat burning furnaces. *(Not to be taken as advice by Type I diabetics for reasons discussed in the chapter on safety).*

Keto-adaptation – The process of converting the body from a carb preferred engine to one that predominantly uses fats as fuel – this often takes a few weeks in a state of Nutritional Ketosis. One of the key goals of being on a Keto diet is to become Keto-adapted.

Once Keto-adapted the body can return to a state of Ketosis more quickly after an inadvertent carb blowout.

Keto-Acidosis – This is a dangerous place to be and along with some other criteria, occurs when Ketone levels are too high such as greater than 10mM. This is more commonly a problem in Type I diabetics, and alcoholics not tracking and adjusting appropriately.

There is no reason or benefits to aim for a Ketone level of greater than 3.0mM and efforts should be made to stay within the parameters of Nutritional Ketosis.

WHAT IS KETOSIS?

When Dr. Atkins's *Diet Revolution* appeared in 1972, the term Ketosis became part of the overall discussion of a healthy diet. His findings showed that when the body is in a state of Ketosis, it is more efficient at converting fats to energy.

In the absence of alternative fuels such as glucose, a natural metabolic action occurs inside your body, breaking down the fats that we eat into a combination of fatty acids and Ketones to use for fuel.

With lower blood sugar and insulin levels it becomes easier for your body to access fat stores to use as fuel.

Ketones that are produced from fats start supplying more and more of your energy requirements, and as their presence increases you enter into a state of Ketosis.

Being in Ketosis gives you more efficient cellular energy, affects insulin levels and studies regarding the therapeutic effects of using Ketones as the bodies primary fuel have revealed a plethora of advantages far surpassing just weight loss.

In fact in a 3 month study[10] by Dr. Jeff Volek of 40 subjects comparing a low carbohydrate diet to one of low fats, the Ketogenic diet showed lower glucose levels, better lipids overall (especially triglyceride results), with improvements in insulin sensitivity, leptin levels, both cholesterol LDL and HDL and saturated fat levels.

Even better, Ketogenic diets have been attributed to health benefits associated with serious disorders such as diabetes, cancer, cardiovascular problems and neuroprotective illnesses such as epilepsy, Alzheimer's, Parkinson's, autism, depression, migraines and so on.

Ketones also promote gut health and are an alternative brain fuel, good for cognitive function and remaining in a state of Nutritional Ketosis may even mimic the effects of caloric restriction, promoting longevity.

HOW ABOUT NUTRITIONAL KETOSIS?

In the years since Dr. Atkins's death, the term Nutritional Ketosis has come into use.

Nutritional Ketosis is the optimal range* of Ketone levels (between **0.5 and 3 mM**) in our blood stream to most safely garner the benefits of a state of Ketosis.

To be more specific between **0.5–1.5 mM** would be considered light Nutritional Ketosis and should have a positive effect on your weight.

Between **1.5-3.0mM** is optimal for maximum weight loss, sparing muscles and supplying us with energy.

There is no reason to seek a higher value than **3.0mM**, results won't improve above the optimal range.

*Note: If you are Type I diabetic however, chasing after higher blood Ketones in an effort to lose weight is not worth the risk. High blood sugar combined with high blood Ketones with a low level of insulin if you are Type I diabetic can lead to Keto-acidosis, a life threatening condition.

HOW DO I MONITOR MY KETONE LEVEL?

Nutritional Ketosis is achieved by having between 0.5mM and 3.0mM in the blood stream, but how do we know when we are within these parameters?

There are several ways to measure for Ketone levels and some are more effective than others.

The most common method of testing is by dipping test strips in collected urine and gauging the color of the stick as to your level of Ketosis. Urinating is non-invasive, quick and easy and is widely regarded as the go-to method of determining if you are in a state of Ketosis or not.

The downside of this method of testing is that once you have been in Ketosis for a while, your kidneys make some adjustments and secrete less of the Ketones detected by the strips. In other words the **ratio** of the types of Ketones in your blood and urine at this point change and the prevalent one is not the type that the urine strips are looking for, which poses the question of how they are still providing an accurate level.

So what can happen is within a few weeks into your Keto diet you'll likely end up confused by the readings on the strips as to why they indicate you are slipping out of Ketosis, when in actual fact you may not be.

This can be discouraging to say the least, so in my opinion, I'd exercise caution when it comes to relying solely on urine test strips as a long-term reliable source of Ketone monitoring.

However, if you are **new** to a Ketogenic diet, using urine strips for the first few weeks should be fine as a reasonably accurate tracking tool, and then after that I suggest looking at other methods of cross-referencing your progress.

One thing to ask yourself before we continue is how important is it really to be tracking all the time?

If you are only eating around 30g of carbs or less per day, and you can taste funky smelling acetone in your mouth, then in all likelihood you are already doing a pretty good job of quantifying that you are in a state of Nutritional Ketosis.

Then again, there are many reasons to look for a more detailed answer, plain and simple curiosity amongst them. I for one, just love data, so I really like to know how deep I'm in Ketosis at any point. If there is a gadget to be bought that can tell me this then I kind of need to have it.

Another reason is that you may have a medical condition that requires your constant attention (especially when experimenting with your diet), such as diabetes, where balancing insulin related medicine with Ketosis can be seriously important for reasons such as avoiding Keto-acidosis.

Aside from urine testing, the two other readily available options are blood testing and acetone testing.

The first is invasive, in that it requires a lancet finger prick and a drop of blood using a handheld glucometer, and there is an expense for each test.

When the necessity is there for the accuracy of measuring serum levels of Ketones, the invasive test and cost pays off and gives peace of mind.

The second option is reasonably new on the circuit, and relies on detecting acetone levels in the breath.

To determine the reliability of this method, a 2014 study[11] was conducted with 99 patients by BioMed Research International and the conclusion was that **exhaled acetone significantly correlated with concentrations of Ketones in the blood and urine**.

When detecting acetone levels, instead of measuring in mM, a device measures PPM (parts of acetone per million parts of air) to determine Ketosis.

Testing for acetone in the breath has a few advantages over the other methods.

It's a non-invasive method of detecting Ketosis in comparison to puncturing yourself for blood.

This technology is only just now emerging as a commercially available testing mechanism and as such most devices are in their first incarnation, although there is one that I recommend and own called a Ketonix which is available online[12].

The Ketonix was originally released as a standard version that when you breathed into it, displayed a light, different in color depending on the level of acetone detected in your breath.

The newer Sports model takes it one step further, and flashes the colored light a certain number of times to let you know more accurately where **within the range** of that level you are, a couple of flashes meaning you are nearer to the acetone level below, and many flashes meaning you are almost at the level above.

Studies are being done to more precisely determine the relationship between PPM acetone levels and how this correlates to mM in the blood. Data is still being collected, although anecdotally from my own testing, when the Ketonix turns green or yellow for me this correlates with my glucometer to indicate that I'm in a state of Nutritional Ketosis. Your tests may yield varying results.

For most lovers of living Keto, this method of testing is an easy to use, accurate tool allowing easy tracking of a state of Nutritional Ketosis without any need to give up bodily fluids like urine and blood.

The best thing of all is an acetone breath device is reusable over and over again with no need to purchase strips thus eliminating recurring costs.

For others with need for serum tracking such as diabetics who need to be mindful of conditions such as Keto-acidosis, blood readings continue to be essential and irreplaceable.

A F.A.Q. ON THE SAFETY AND CONCERNS ABOUT FAT FASTING

How long can I continue a Fat Fast safely?

The Fat Fast is designed to be attempted by insulin and metabolically resistant people on a plateau and is not an eating plan or a diet for the long term. Dr. Atkins suggested 3 to 5 days though some studies and personal anecdotal reports claims of up to a week of Fat Fasting with no negative consequences.

When you fast, your body typically responds by turning to all the stored energy sources available to satisfy its needs depleting glycogen and then turning to fat stores and proteins in our muscles.

A Fat Fast is not the same as a total zero calorie fast. Your body is still receiving 1000 calories of fuel each day and the studies discussed earlier in the book show this to be better for sparing muscle than a total fast.

However a Fat Fast is still a caloric level less than what your body normally requires and not sustainable.

Our body needs protein to survive and build tissue, and after a certain point caloric restriction coupled with limited dietary protein results in not getting the appropriate variety and quantity of nutrients and essential amino acids.

However, for a period of 3-5 days, a Fat Fast may be the perfect antidote to your plateau or to nudge your metabolism into Nutritional Ketosis, after which time I recommend returning to a more suitable caloric intake along with increased protein consumption.

And though you'll be getting some calories, as a rule, you should always begin any dietary change, even for a short period of time, with general medical expert advice on any benefits or perils that directly relate to your own personal current health condition.

Is a Fat Fast safe for diabetics (or those with hypoglycaemia) on insulin or blood sugar lowering medicine?

The short answer here is NO, not without medical supervision.

Anyone currently taking insulin or blood-sugar-lowering medications, whether you are diagnosed with diabetes or have another condition requiring this should be extremely careful when considering embarking on a Fat Fast.

The safest thing for me to suggest if you are on these medications is to avoid going on a Fat Fast completely. Why? On a Fat Fast your blood sugar drops fast and this means you will be requiring constant monitoring and supervision in order to properly regulate and adjust accordingly the medications that help manage blood sugar and insulin levels.

It is critical that this is not ignored, as side effects such as insulin shock or diabetic Ketoacidosis that can occur caused by incorrect blood glucose levels can have fatal consequences.

With all of that said, if you have the support of your doctor who can medically supervise you, your intake levels of your medication, and can regularly monitor your progress throughout, then and only then, you might consider attempting a program such as this with greater confidence.

Aren't all those saturated fats from meats and dairy going to clog my arteries?

There's been a lot of talk about fats in the past few decades. The message that seems to have stuck with the general public is that all fats are bad, with saturated fats the worst.

Yet a review of numerous studies points out that there is no link between eating saturated fats and increased levels of atherosclerosis (hardening of the arteries) and heart disease. In actual fact some studies show that decreasing saturated fats in favor of increasing carbohydrates actually **increases** the risk of coronary conditions.

When US scientist, Dr. Ancel Keys studied the diets of the world, and wrote about the correlation between heart disease and fat intake in the 1950's, one regional diet wasn't co-operating in line with the conclusions drawn in other countries.

One of the challenges he had was finding a good explanation for reasons that The Mediterranean Diet (followed in Crete), was so high in fat yet had such excellent health benefits replete with far lower rates of cardiovascular disease, when compared to diets in other parts of the world such as the United States where fat consumption seemed to have so many negative health issues attributed to it.

It was a paradox that seemed to fly directly in all of the dietary theory of the time.

In an era when margarine and shortening were seen as healthier alternatives to butter and lard, the message was hard to process. In the end, the explanation presented argued that the **type** of fat used in the Mediterranean diet (olive oil), was a source of mono-unsaturated fats, and this bit of sleight of hand helped support popular hypothesis that saturated fats were the bad ones.

However, with olive oil also containing 14% saturated fats, many scientists saw this as requiring further examination.

Deeper studies into the Mediterranean diet demonstrated additional benefits, such as longer life expectancy, protection from Type 2 diabetes, and reduced risk of cancer, cardiovascular disease, Parkinson's and Alzheimer's.

Another example, (the French Paradox) surrounds the observation that the French consume a diet fairly high in saturated fats, yet also have a relatively low rate of incidences of coronary heart diseases.

This too implied that the hypothesis surrounding links between saturated fats and heart disease is simply put... invalid.

And further studies of fattier diets continued to yield positive results.

A 2008 study[13] from The New England Journal of Medicine went so far as to pit three diets alongside each other – a Low Fat Diet, the Mediterranean Diet and a Low Carbohydrate Diet. **Interestingly, the low-carb diet was responsible for the greatest weight loss, and resulted in the most favourable changes in blood lipids overall.** The Mediterranean diet came second, with the low fat diet in last place.

In fact a meta-analysis of 21 studies in 2010[14] conceded there was **no significant evidence to conclude dietary saturated fats are associated with an increased risk of coronary heart or vascular disease** at all!

And another meta-analysis in 2014 of 32 studies with over half a million participants[15] concluded **that current evidence does not clearly support cardiovascular guidelines that encourage low consumption of total saturated fats**.

There are so many studies on this, including the excellent study on blood lipids by Dr. Jeff Volek which actually detected **less saturated fats in found in triacylglycerol *after* subjects completed a high fat diet**.

I would encourage you to research further.

Am I worried about eating fat in my own diet? No. As long as I'm not eating them in conjunction with a bunch of high GI carbs, I'm completely ok with it.

Won't so much fat increase my cholesterol?

The evidence to prove that dietary cholesterol, in the form of animal foods and fats (saturated fats), causes cardiovascular disease, heart attacks or stroke is again, lacking to say the least.

Following on from the studies presented in the previous section, another study[16] in 2006 of 66 obese individuals placed on a Ketogenic diet for 56 weeks had an outcome resulting in a decrease in total cholesterol, the *bad* LDL cholesterol, triglycerides and blood glucose levels and a significant increase in the *good* HDL cholesterol.

There are other consistent studies that support the conclusion that eating low-carb and staying Keto if anything, **improves** your lipid profile and overall heart health.

Digging deeper, it's also been argued that the only real factor to consider when it comes to cholesterol measuring is how many LDL *particles* you have, with a lower amount being better. And it's good to know, studies show that LDL particle count is also improved on a carb restricted diet.

Is there a fat preference?

Actually, yes.

All foods that contain fat actually contain a mixture of 3 fats. Saturated fats (SFA), Mono-unsaturated fats (MUFA), and Poly-unsaturated fats (PUFA).

The fat we should eat the least of is PUFA, a fat commonly found in corn oils.

PUFA has a skewed omega-6 to omega-3 ratio of around 20:1 instead of the preferable 2:1 or 1:1 ratio, so when choosing oils and food types containing fats, PUFA should be a less favourable *dominating* fat choice in preference of more MUFA and SFA heavy options.

MUFA and SFA are found in fats such as butter coconut and olive oils, sour cream, eggs, avocado and macadamias, bacon and pepperoni – it's worth your time to look into this a little more when making your food choices.

And trans-fats not occurring naturally, and ersatz (fake) fats made from processed and highly refined hydrogenated oils are associated with medical risks, and should be avoided. Margarine, shortening, and butter replacements for example are not considered *healthy* fats, nor should be on a well put together Keto diet.

Don't I need plenty of glucose to fuel my brain?

Great question. It's definitely worth discussing this further because as it turns out, the brain is a hungry little fella, always thinking, synapses firing and burning up calories.

In fact even though the brain's weight accounts for only 2 percent of our total weight, it accounts for **20 percent** of our daily caloric quota, and usually demands glucose as its primary source of fuel, which comes primarily from carbohydrates, and also through a process known as gluconeogenesis from protein.

When beginning a Ketogenic diet, voluntarily decreasing carbohydrates and increasing fats, after a while our urine gets a little funky, and our breath starts to feel like the acetone fairy has arrived. At this point we have likely entered a state of Nutritional Ketosis, which as covered earlier, we can test using various methods and technologies.

In this state, with a shortage of available glucose, an alternative source of fuel is sought by the hungry grey matter.

Turning to Ketones, some interesting changes take place upstairs including the way the brain handles key amino-acids, GABA (inhibitory) and glutamate (excitatory).

Essentially, the ratio of these gets changed up causing an increase in GABA.

This is thought to be a good thing, as over-excited neurons can die. In fact if the ratio is too glutamate heavy, incidences of seizures, strokes and various neurodegenerative disorders are more prevalent.

So for example, if we consider epilepsy, it is thought that a Ketone operating brain has an amino-acid balance that makes neuron membranes harder to excite, ultimately causing a higher seizure threshold, making it harder to reach that *seizure moment*, which is of course, a good thing.

It seems to me that what is being discovered is the brain is having a much more relaxed time of things on Ketones.

Let's dig deeper!

When we pull out the microscope and take a look inside mitochondria (our brains energy factories), after glucose has been through our system, there's a lot of leftover garbage still there in comparison to after Ketones have paid a visit.

Producing energy using Ketones, with less free radicals to clean up afterwards, makes for a more efficient energy.

Not only this, but it turns out that a Keto diet actually also **increases the number** of mitochondria in the learning and memory part of the brain, the hippocampus. More energy factories mean increased energy reserves which may also be attributed to helping neurons resist disease.

With more studies coming to light demonstrating improvements in sleep and bipolar disorders, autism, neurodegenerative diseases, brain cancer and even headaches, the neuro-protective effects of a brain operating on Ketones are becoming more and more apparent.

For instance, a study[17] of several patients with Parkinson's disease on a Ketogenic diet showed a reduction in symptoms; a study of elderly people showed a demonstrable improvement in memory performance compared to a high carb diet; and a study[18] of patients with Alzheimer's showed a marked cognitive improvement when on a Ketogenic diet.

These are such hope filled results for anyone with a neurological disorder.

It's true that the brain is still a mystery and a great deal of things are going on when we switch to Ketones as a fuel source for the brain. And yes, a lot of studies are fairly new, or still emerging.

Yet it seems that from looking at an analysis of current studies, fuelling a brain with Ketones doesn't appear to be associated with any observably negative side effects.

The future sure looks promising for Keto.

What exactly the full extent of cognitive enhancements, anti-inflammatory and anti-oxidative properties, mood stability, and neuro-protective benefits will prove to be is a fascinating work in progress.

So if you're asking me if it's ok to run our brains on Ketones, my personal opinion is… another slice of cheese please!

Should I worry about sodium, potassium and magnesium intake on a Ketogenic diet?

Yes! It's important to stay topped up.

If you are reading this you may have heard about the dreaded Keto flu!

During your first days on a Ketogenic diet, and perhaps even the first couple of weeks, your body is withdrawing from its dependence on carbohydrates and learning to use Ketones as a preferred fuel.

This brain fog and fatigue may feel a bit like a flu, and is expected. Hang in there and take some electrolytes!

With insulin levels decreasing, the message to your kidneys to retain sodium also decreases and the metabolic changes and diuretic effects you experience on Keto mean you'll be flushing a lot of sodium, and also potassium and magnesium from your body.

All of these electrolytes are however important for health and this includes cardiovascular health.

Luckily there's quite a bit of these in some of our favorite Keto foods, such as the sodium found in bacon and potassium in avocados.

Again, for most people, adding salt to a diet is something that feels counter-intuitive.

Instead of worrying we are adding too much salt to our food, we suddenly find ourselves needing to make sure we are getting enough, and should in fact be aiming for around 2 grams of sodium a day.

Table salt is 40% sodium, so that's around 5 grams of salt.

In addition to this, aim for around a **minimum** of a gram a day of potassium to avoid cramping (USRDA is actually more than this, as much as 3.5g depending on the individual), and 300mg of magnesium. These three electrolytes will go a long way towards making you feel better.

You may even find that Keto actually lowers your blood pressure. However, for some added peace of mind, if you **are** prone to blood pressure issues and still worried about sodium intake due to a sensitivity, check with your doctor and test your blood pressure regularly while on a Keto diet using an at home device to ensure you aren't overshooting what your body can handle comfortably.

What about kidney and liver function during a Fat Fast?

A Fat Fast is so short that fears about causing damage to internal organs are reasonably unfounded so let's talk about these concerns for a Ketogenic diet in general.

Firstly, there's not a lot I have to say about the liver.

By most accounts, fatty liver disease is caused by carbs, with time spent on a Ketogenic diet actually improving this condition. Also there is a lot of research to indicate that saturated fats are shown to improve alcoholic liver injuries. On a related note, assuming you are not malnourished and drinking excessively, alcoholic specific Ketoacidosis should not be a concern.

The subject of whether Keto will hurt your kidneys is a little more involved, and the short answer is that for most of us, there is no need to worry.

A 2012 study[19] of 307 obese adults with *no existing serious illness* was conducted to examine the effects of a low-carbohydrate, high-protein diet on the kidneys.

The conclusion was that in healthy obese individuals, consumption of this diet over 2 years was not associated with any noticeable harmful renal effects.

While the criteria of this study did not exactly match that of a Ketogenic profile, the results speak for themselves.

If we want to get into nuts and bolts over and above that study, let's examine the effects of a high protein diet on an *already deteriorated kidney*.

What we **do** know is that higher protein intake goes through a process that ultimately ends up in increased urine acidity.

For those with an existing chronic kidney disease (which can affect the rate of uric acid excretion), eating a diet that consists of too much protein may be cause for concern.

An increase in uric acid is accompanied by a decrease in levels of citrate which when not properly excreted, increases the risk of kidney stone formation.

For those prone to kidney stones, especially in relation to a hereditary condition, this higher uric acid can present a problem.

Supplementation of citrates (calcium, magnesium and potassium citrates) goes a long way towards keeping kidney stones at bay.

Proper hydration and drinking water in general at the levels recommended in this book is another great way to keep the kidneys flushed.

Eating alkalizing vegetables also helps to offset the acidity Ketones and excess protein can present.

Personally, I find that simply eating non-starchy vegetables and drinking enough water is enough for me. Another reason I don't worry to excess, is that a Keto diet is not really a high protein diet, it's a high fat diet. *Some* of the above concerns surround high protein intake however the acidic effect from an increase in Ketones can in some individuals, remain a consideration.

If you have no existing kidney condition, or history of such in your family, I wouldn't overthink it too much.

However if you do have further concerns, you should elect to discuss them with your doctor. And you may also like to keep track of the pH levels in your urine with test strips if this gives you greater peace of mind.

Will I be hungry on the Fat Fast?

Every person experiences this differently. It's tempting to downplay this as I know from experience that if you do suffer from an initial ravenous bump in the road, things tend to get better quickly.

But this shouldn't be minimized as cravings and hunger can and have derailed even the most dedicated of us.

How **you** will fare depends on a couple of things. In many ways the severity of a hunger reaction in the early stages of a Fat Fast largely depends on your experience with eating a low carbohydrate Ketogenic diet so far.

As we've gone over several times in the book so far, the recommendation is that a Fat Fast should be attempted after first stalling on a Ketogenic diet, and even then, after spending a few weeks testing you have in fact experienced a stall and are not simply off track.

However, if you've put this advice on the sidelines, are completely new to living Keto and you're still attempting to jump head first into a Fat Fast anyway, then be aware that the rapid shift from a regular diet of high carbohydrate foods will almost certainly leave you feeling grumbly in the stomach, foggy and fatigued.

Cravings are psychological in their origin making you feel distracted and anxious while you long for the feeling of *forbidden* foods in your mouth, and these moments can even feel quite physical during this swift transition to low-carb eating.

And like an addict trying to kick a habit, you may have to go through an uncomfortable period of going *cold turkey*.

Of course, in this case, it would be a little bit of cold turkey with a lot of mayonnaise, but you get the idea. You may have to tough it out for a period of time. However don't worry. If this *is* the case, in time your body will eventually stop looking for the quick fuel that isn't there anymore and will stop signalling your brain you need carbs to fill up the tanks quickly.

Your insulin levels will balance out, that peculiar empty feeling will go away and instead of having cravings that rage out of control you'll find that your appetite and feelings of hunger begin to moderate.

For some people, the Fat Fast is actually the means to an end. And that end is breaking their cravings.

Best of all, you will finally have the perspective necessary to determine when you are truly hungry.

If however, you are entering a Fat Fast after a few weeks on an induction diet, where carbohydrates have been already limited, it is far less likely that you will suffer any serious hunger for very long as elevated Ketones thankfully have the effect of dampening an appetite.

In fact many people who experience cravings report that the sensation they found so overwhelming at the start of a Fat Fast diminished after twenty-four hours or so, as they started to fall in to a sustained state of deeper Nutritional Ketosis and fat burning.

In those initial couple of days though, if you **do** experience any small amount of hunger, simply stay busy, spread out your meals and look forward to the benefits ahead as the Ketones do their job. A Fat Fast is not forever. You'll do just fine.

The other kind of craving is for a certain texture or flavor. I've worked hard to ensure that the recipes ahead contain a selection that should cover even the most demanding of desires!

GUIDELINES

The Fat Fast guidelines are as follows.

1. Restrict total calories to no more than 1000 a day (this includes both food and beverages).

2. 90% of caloric value should consist of fats.

3. This should be broken up into four to five *feedings*, around 200-250 calories each, spaced about 2 to 3 hours apart, or when you feel actual physical hunger.

4. The Fat Fast is complete after 3-5 days.

FLEXIBILITY ON THE DIET MECHANICS

The best laid schemes of mice and men oft go awry...

This well-known quote from Robert Burns in 1785 sums it up.

At some point you may find yourself standing in your kitchen agonizing over a tablespoon of cream, biting your nails about overshooting your calorie quota by a couple of hundred for the day.

Don't let it get to you.

Give yourself a buffer. You really won't do any drastic harm to the overall effectiveness of the diet by moving the thresholds a little bit.

So I propose this. Firstly do your best to stay within the guidelines. Secondly, ignore what I just said and revise your outer limits a little to make sure you stay **at the very least** within 1200 calories a day, with 80% of those calories from fats.

Listen to your body and adjust meal portions and the timing of each to best suit your hunger.

Don't be too worried by a little flexibility short circuiting your hard work.

In reality, you are unlikely to go under 80% fat from your calories. All of the recipes in this book have at **least** 80% fat calories, some more than 90%. The overall **average** fat calories of your meals will be well above 80%, I'm certain.

Watching that calorie limit is a little trickier but not too much. Portion sizes, drinking a lot of water and perhaps eating some voluminous low calorie foods such as broth, or shirataki noodles all help. Side orders of will power and keeping distracted are good too.

I apologize if I sound overly dramatic – you really won't starve. You'll still be eating something, and fats are very filling so I'm sure you'll be just fine.

And if you get to the very end of the day and you find yourself still hungry, that's when you reach for that bowl of sugar free gelatin in the fridge. (You did make a bowl of gelatin didn't you?). Sure it's not very creative, but it takes a while to eat, has barely any calories and comes with the added Keto benefits of glycine intake. (Even better with whipped cream, calories permitting).

GETTING READY FOR A FAT FAST

A Fat Fast should rarely be the first step in trying to encourage your body to start burning fat.

Living Keto, following a high-fat, medium-protein, and restricted-carbohydrate plan may be all your body needs.

And as previously covered, attempting a Ketogenic lifestyle for three or four weeks first is recommended before starting a Fat Fast. I would even go as far to say that a Fat Fast should only be considered after a stall or plateau in weight loss can be quantifiably verified over the course of a few weeks.

Another excellent reason to follow that advice concerns cravings. When you go directly from a high-carbohydrate diet to a Ketogenic one, you will initially experience cravings for familiar foods like pasta and bread and sugar.

You should spend some time letting your body adjust to using Ketones for fuel before you throw in the calorie restrictions of a Fat Fast.

Also, consider your motivation. If your plan is simply to drop a few pounds and then go back to the *status quo* of a conventional non-Ketogenic diet, you might be setting yourself up for a cycle of yo-yo dieting, with all of its attendant health consequences. A commitment to a better, healthier lifestyle is more significant than looking good for a photograph.

With all of this in mind, if you are already following a Ketogenic diet and you are hitting hurdles along the way, then it may be time to consider a Fat Fast to get past your weight loss plateau, break through the persistent cycle of cravings, and reach a more effective state of Ketosis.

Enough with the precautions, if you've read everything so far and this is for you, let's get in to it.

Here's the plan...

The best preparation boils down to three key strategies:

- Pick your time to suit your life and your schedule.
- Have a plan for the days you are going to spend on the Fat Fast.
- Stock your kitchen and refrigerator for your Fat Fast.

PICK YOUR TIME

Try to do your Fat Fast when you can be relatively certain you won't be going to parties or out to eat with friends and family. For example, try starting on a Sunday morning and finishing on a Tuesday or Wednesday night.

Of course, someone well-seasoned in the art of living Keto isn't usually daunted by the prospect of a mere party or social gathering, whatever the day of the week – the willpower to avoid carbs is ingrained into the system!

When out and about, we order our burritos naked (meaning without the tortilla, not actually whilst naked). We get the fish, but leave the chips, and one way or another we are able to sit alongside our carb consuming brethren, doing our best not to push our Keto beliefs onto them, all the while knowing what we know and biting our tongue (well at least I try, although I'm always happy to share to whoever asks!).

Sound familiar?

Unfortunately, even though we do our best not to shove **our** lifestyle down the throats of others, that courtesy is not always reciprocated.

"Piece of cake? You really should, it's Andy's birthday. Come on..."

These days when I visit friends, I just take something along that I've prepared from my own recipes and munch alongside everyone else.

Yet even with this line of defence, on a Fat Fast going on social outings may make it harder to keep your calorie count low or to find the right Fat Fast foods you need whilst away from your kitchen.

If you do hit the town, you'll quickly realize that 1000 calories isn't a lot, so when heading out to an event that entails eating, or to places you habitually graze, such as the cinema (nom, nom - nuts and pork rinds), succumbing to temptation or improper tracking is likely to steer you off course.

So pick a time you can focus on yourself.

You may like to let anyone you live with know what you are doing, especially if you'll be eating with them and your meal and portions will be different to theirs.

Regarding exercise, there is no need to make any drastic changes to a regime that includes a brisk walk or a light workout. Any more than this, be aware you'll be consuming less calories, and will be glycogen depleted.

If your body is already familiar with using Ketones for fuel this may not be a problem.

If not, you may lack in performance or energy exerting yourself too much so when in doubt, listen to your body and don't overdo yourself during this time.

HAVE AN EATING PLAN

You are most likely still wondering how the whole Fat Fast works on a practical level. What does a day's eating plan *look like*? How can you tell if you are eating enough fat and simultaneously not eating too many calories?

With the calorie and fat calculated recipes contained in this book, it's easy to prepare a few sample menus you can adhere to. There is no special magic in having foods in a specific sequence, so if you'd rather save a *breakfast* style feeding for later in the day, that's your prerogative.

An example day might look something like this:-

> 8am – **Cheese and Mushroom Soufflé Omelet** (221 calories, 83% fat) – 183
>
> 12am – **Herby Puff** (156 Calories, 86% fat) – 129
>
> 3pm - **2 x Coconut Orange fat Bombs** (200 Calories, 95% fat) - 190
>
> 6pm – **Creamy Mushroom Soup** (244 Calories, 87% fat) - 213
>
> 7pm – **Yogurt Cheesecake** (264 Calories, 87% fat) – 230
>
> **Final count – Calories 1085, Calories from fat 945 (87%)**

One less Orange fat Bomb would have been a little stricter, sure, but what the hell.

Your own daily menu will undoubtedly vary and if you are being slightly more flexible with calories your portion sizes may also shift a little, but overall, this is a pretty good example of a Fat Fast day with an interesting selection of flavors throughout.

Oh, and regarding drinks on this sample day, just drink water liberally. Tea or black coffee is also fine and diet soda is good but better still if you can get the Stevia / Erythritol brands.

Your daily plan may even prefer to switch up one of your meals for a fat infused coffee, such as the Intrepid Coffee found in Keto Living 3.

Keep it interesting and you may find it hard to believe you're even on a diet!

For even more variety, at the end of this book I have listed all the recipes you can discover in my other cookbooks that are also suitable to enjoy on a Fat Fast.

STOCK YOUR KITCHEN AND REFRIGERATOR

Likely, you have already been on a Keto diet for some time so many of the ingredients we need will already be on your shelves.

Check which recipes you think you'll try before the Fat Fast begins, and make a shopping list for the entire period of any ingredients you don't already have. That will keep you out of the grocery store and away from external temptation during the Fat Fast.

In the next section we will journey through many of the kinds of higher fat foods you'll be able to enjoy on a Fat Fast and a couple of my notes on each.

SO WHAT EXACTLY WILL I BE EATING?

If you've heard about the Fat Fast before, then you've possibly also heard about the two foods described as near perfect for our criteria, macadamia nuts and cream cheese.

Yet although these two foods fit the macronutrient profile, and as delicious as a handful of nuts can be, you are right in wondering if even for a few days such a limited *menu* is sustainable.

By now I expect you've glanced at the recipes in the Table of Contents, and looked at the Sample Menu from a couple of pages ago, and hopefully you are starting to realize that there can be a lot more versatility on a Fat Fast than you thought.

With just a little care in the kitchen and some flourish with a spice here and some zest there, you'll soon have your fears put to rest.

Also, in the Appendix at the end of this book I list **all** the recipes you can find in the other Keto Living cookbooks that are suitable for a Fat Fast. If you have access to these, that will more double the recipe choices available to you to keep satisfied.

So what are the many other foods that you can enjoy? What are the best tactics to combine low-calorie, low-carbohydrate foods with very high-fat foods in a way that will boost your organoleptic experience and keep you from jumping ship in frustration.

In this section we'll look at foods and beverages that suit our needs for you to have a successful Fat Fast.

Some of the foods listed in the pages ahead are not used in the recipes to follow but are instead mentioned so if you elect to head off the beaten path into uncharted experimental cooking at some stage (always recommended), you'll have a good idea of which foods fall pretty close the 90% fat mark and are better suited for a Fat Fast.

MEATS AND POULTRY: ANIMAL FATS

Once upon a time, cooks around the world kept a refrigerated jar of drippings close at hand. Whatever the fat, whether from a roast bird or piece of salt pork for stew, into the jar it went.

I guess people got out of that habit following questionable advice that saturated fats do horrible things to our bodies.

I'm not suggesting we bring back the dripping jar, we can easily get plenty of fresh fats from the butcher.

Listed below, are various types of **Meat** with their fat content to help you select the fattiest cuts!

Meats and seafood that are lower in fat content such as chicken, shrimp, ham etc. that are not mentioned in the below list are still useful on a Fat Fast if other ingredients can be combined in a recipe to make up the balance of fats.

I would like to note that this will be the least accurate section due to such variables as the difference in fat content of cuts of meat, whether meat is prepared with skin on or without, the method of cooking, and so on.

Based on that, I'm choosing to get this section out of the way first and for what it is worth, all of the below cuts are based on raw fatty cuts, with the skin left on where applicable.

Food	Serving size	Calories	Fat %
Pork Belly	1 oz. (28g)	147	92%
Bacon	1 oz. (28g)	117	83%
Ground Beef (30% fat)	1 oz. (28g)	93	82%
Pepperoni	1 oz. (28g)	138	80%
Beef Short Ribs	1 oz. (28g)	133	81%
Pork sausage	1 oz. (28g)	86	79%
Duck (with skin)	1 oz. (28g)	115	73%
Bologna (beef and pork)	1 oz. (28g)	87	72%
Pork Spareribs	1 oz. (28g)	81	72%
Lamb (ground)	1 oz. (28g)	80	66%
Chicken Wing (with skin)	1 oz. (28g)	63	65%
Atlantic Salmon	1 oz. (28g)	59	56%

EGGS

Eggs and egg yolks can be part of a Fat Fast, with some additions. They **are** higher in fat compared to other foods, however in a Fat Fast they'll need some extra fats added to get closer to that 90% fat content we are aiming for.

Cooking an egg in butter or oil, or scrambling it with some cream and cheese then serving with a little avocado are the kind of easy adjustments you can make to boost calories and fats enough to make a 200-250 calorie feeding out of a yummy egg.

Food	Serving size	Calories	Fat %
Eggs yolks	2 large (34g)	110	74%
Eggs, whole	2 large (100g)	146	60%

DAIRY FATS

I'm a huge fan of **Dairy**, especially butter! Truly, why anyone would still eat margarine is beyond me. Oh, that's right. Because we were told by the powers that be it was "butter" for us. Why is so much misinformation still being "spread" around? (Sorry for the bad puns, I'll show myself out).

Whole butter is composed of around 99% fat calories consisting of about 80% butterfat combined with some milk proteins and water. European-style butters have an even greater ratio of butterfat which is great for baking. Boasting a rich, satisfying flavor, butter is an indispensable food for adding flavor, texture, and of course fat, to many foods.

Oh... and salted or unsalted? That depends on whether you want greater control of the salty flavor in the finished product!

Cream, sour cream and crème fraiche, are other great dairy choices for a Fat Fast. Read labels to be sure you are buying full-fat and that there aren't any added starches and stabilizers (reduced fat and non-fat versions typically include them).

Food	Serving size	Calories	Fat %
Butter	1 oz. (28g)	204	99%
Crème fraîche	1 oz. (28g)	110	90%
Heavy cream	1 oz. (28g)	103	96%
Sour cream	1 oz. (28g)	61	86%

Yogurt, full fat Greek-style	1 oz. (28g)	33	65%

CHEESES

People interested in slimming have been told to stay away from cheeses for decades.

Phooey to that!

Cheese is a high in fat and being able to enjoy a good cheese is one of the best things about Keto. In fact, cream cheese by its very profile, is historically a cornerstone in most Fat Fast regimes.

So how about it? Do you fancy some cheese? How about a little Red Leicester? Some Wensleydale or perhaps some Norwegian Jarlsberg, per chance?

(Forgive my digression into a Monty Python reference – their classic cheese shop skit warrants a little fromage... err... homage)

Moving right along... some of the cheeses listed below may actually not be fatty enough for a Fat Fast eaten on their own. Many are in fact less than 80% in fat content, but are perfectly fine in the right recipe with some extra fats to tip the ratio such as with a bit of butter or sour cream. The main thing to take away is that although cream cheese is the go-to cheese on a Fat Fast, there **are** other options available to you if cream cheese just isn't your thing.

Here's a few examples.

Food	Serving size	Calories	Fat %
Mascarpone	1 oz. (28g)	127	91%
Cream Cheese	1 oz. (28g)	97	90%
Monterey Jack	1 oz. (28g)	107	81%
American (Slice)	1 oz. (28g)	105	75%
Brie	1 oz. (28g)	95	75%
Roquefort	1 oz. (28g)	105	75%
Bleu	1 oz. (28g)	100	74%
Cheddar	1 oz. (28g)	114	74%
Chèvre (Goat Cheese)	1 oz. (28g)	103	74%

Camembert	1 oz. (28g)	85	73%
Gorgonzola	1 oz. (28g)	99	73%
Feta	1 oz. (28g)	75	72%
Gruyère	1 oz. (28g)	117	71%
Gouda	1 oz. (28g)	101	70%
Provolone	1 oz. (28g)	100	68%
Velveeta	1 oz. (28g)	81	68%
Mozzarella (Whole Milk)	1 oz. (28g)	85	67%
Swiss	1 oz. (28g)	108	66%
Parmesan	1 oz. (28g)	128	56%
Ricotta	1 oz. (28g)	39	51%

NUTS

Nuts are high energy, nutrient-dense foods. When on a Fat Fast, it is important not to overshoot your calories, so if you're feeling lazy and just grabbing a handful of nuts for a feed, take the extra time to measure out your portion properly, using a scale.

Food	Serving size	Calories	Fat %
Macadamia	1 oz. (28g)	201	93%
Pecan	1 oz. (28g)	193	93%
Brazil	1 oz. (28g)	184	89%
Walnut	1 oz. (28g)	183	87%
Pinenuts	1 oz. (28g)	188	87%
Hazelnuts	1 oz. (28g)	176	86%
Almonds (and almond flour)	1 oz. (28g)	162	78%

Peanuts	1 oz. (28g)	159	76%
Pistachio	1 oz. (28g)	156	72%
Cashew	1 oz. (28g)	155	67%

NUT BUTTERS

There are many different brands of **Nut Butters** out there. Some of them are simply nuts ground to a smooth or crunchy paste and some are mixed with a little oil which increases the fat content. Then there are those that are mixed with starches and other such carbohydrates, which we need to avoid.

The best advice I can give you is to spend some time in the aisles looking at labels, and reading ingredients. It's actually a great habit to get into.

One particular nut butter that you'll see I've included in several recipes is coconut butter.

As I'll cover in the next section, coconut isn't really a nut, but this seems to be the most suitable section to talk about it.

I like to use coconut butter in Fat Fast recipes for its near perfect nutritional profile, and amazing flavors.

In some cases depending on the recipe, you can substitute coconut oil in the recipe, but there's no need, as it's not hard to make. Here, let me help.

HOW TO MAKE YOUR OWN COCONUT BUTTER

1. Blend shredded, unsweetened coconut for around 5-10 minutes. Double that amount of time for a food processor.

There you go! When you have the consistency is that of a smooth thick liquid, that's coconut butter. No need to refrigerate it, it'll keep for a couple of months in a sealed jar in the cupboard.

COCONUT

Are you wondering why **Coconut** has its own section? Well... technically it's not really a nut, or a fruit (so it's been argued).

It's kind of more like a massive seed, or maybe more technically, a drupe. But then again, it doesn't even really fit into that category. Some botanists call it a *dry drupe*. Well, I don't really care if it has trouble finding a category in the literature of lofty plant scientists, all I know is it's magnificent and tastes amazing. So I put it in its own, glorious, nutty, fruity, seedy, drupey section.

With a profile high in saturated fats, coconut is perfect for a Fat Fast full of delicious island flavors. Just remember to stick to the unsweetened stuff!

You can even make your own coconut milk from unsweetened flaked coconut or fresh meat for a healthy and economical option in your Fat Fast. Here's a recipe to get you going!

HOW TO MAKE YOUR OWN COCONUT MILK

1. Heat 4 cups (960ml) of water to a hot (not scalding), temperature.

2. Add the water to about 2 cups (186g) of shredded unsweetened coconut (fresh or dried) into the jar of a blender (the more powerful the better).

3. Puree the coconut and water until it is very smooth and creamy.

4. Strain the milk through a colander to get the larger chunks out of the way, and then again through a fine sieve of doubled cheesecloth, squeezing as much liquid from the pulp as possible.

5. The coconut milk will keep in covered jars in the refrigerator for 3 or 4 days.

6. Some of the coconut cream may rise to the surface as it sits in the refrigerator, just stir it back into the milk before using or drinking or lift it off to use on its own, plain or whipped into a topping.

Food	Serving size	Calories	Fat %
Coconut oil (organic, not refined)	1 oz. (28g)	241	100%
Coconut milk (unsweetened)	1 oz. (28g)	66	94%
Coconut cream (unsweetened)	1 oz. (28g)	94	94%
Coconut butter (pureed meat)	1 oz. (28g)	210	90%
Desiccated coconut (unsweetened)	1 oz. (28g)	187	86%

FATS AND OILS

Almost all **Fats and Oils** (with the exception of mayonnaise), are 100% fat, around 250 calories per ounce (28g).

There's so many ways to use oil. Dress a salad, sauté a piece of meat, or add oil to a Fat Bomb creation.

When we calculate calories from oil in a Fat Fast we need to consider **how** the oil is used. If for example, you are frying something, what is the absorbability of what's being fried? How much is added and how much is burned up or poured out as waste?

It's easy in an oily salad, soup or as part of a Fat Bomb to calculate the caloric total of what's been added, less so in some other dishes. You can be sure that when I prepare my nutritional panels at the bottom of each recipe that I spend a lot of time thinking about how much oil finds its way into each serve in an attempt to provide information that's as close to accurate as possible.

In making a considered choice on **which** oil to choose, we need to know what **type** of fat calorie is best.

As examined earlier we need to favor oils with a lower percentage of poly-unsaturated fats (PUFA). Oils with a higher percentage of PUFA's that can easily be avoided include Canola, Corn, Flaxseed, Grape-seed, Safflower, Sesame, Soybean, and Sunflower. Actually, Peanut and Walnut oils are both high in PUFA's too.

And although it has an ok profile, Palm oil is contentious as Asian plantations encroach upon orangutan habitations, not good at all. It takes careful purchasing to enjoy Palm oil with a clean conscience. Red Palm oil from West Africa is an example where you should be ok. I just avoid it all together.

Your safest option is simply to stick to oils like the ones below. These are abundant and have a great profile.

Food	Serving size	Calories	Fat %
Avocado oil (better for salads than for high heat cooking)	1 oz. (28g)	248	100%
Macadamia nut oil	1 oz. (28g)	248	100%
Olive oil	1 oz. (28g)	248	100%
Coconut oil (organic, not refined)	1 oz. (28g)	241	100%

MAYONNAISE AND VINAIGRETTES

Mayonnaise, a classic cold sauce has a lot going for it. It's creamy, smooth, and ever so slightly tangy. Stirred into a salad, it can boost the percentage of fat up to an acceptable level required on a Fat Fast.

Scratch-made mayonnaise is a sauce of egg yolks, oil, and a little vinegar. Store-bought versions of mayonnaise and salad dressings contain those ingredients too, but they may also contain the very sugars and starches we're trying to avoid, so be careful to check the ingredients before purchasing. Look for *real* mayonnaise and try to buy one that has been made using low PUFA oils as recommended previously.

In a **Vinaigrette**, the traditional ratio is three parts oil to one part vinegar. Adding a generous quantity of this easy-to-make and easy-to-store dressing can also add a good fat ratio to a dish.

Food	Serving size	Calories	Fat %
Mayonnaise (buy one made with a recommended oil)	1 oz. (28g)	200	99%
Vinaigrette (made from 1½ tbsp. oil and ½ tsp. vinegar)	1 oz. (28g)	180	99%

DARK CHOCOLATE

Yes! Even glorious **Dark Chocolate** can even be part of a Fat Fast, if it has a high enough cocoa percentage.

OMG! How is this possible Ella? Well with the magic of science we soon discover that the darkest of chocolates whilst being lower in sweetness also have a nice amount of fat.

Whisk in a dash of stevia, add a little butter, and pretty soon just the right combination of awesome comes together to leave you in a state of astonished disbelief.

With dark chocolate, brands really matter to find just the right window of chocolate possibilities, so reading nutritional panels before you buy is the real trick here. A few percentage points of cocoa makes enough of a difference in macronutrient levels to suggest it's worth chasing the purer stuff.

I haven't listed it here as it's not mainstream and was pretty expensive, but I even stumbled across a brand of delicious dark chocolate this week pre-sweetened with stevia and erythritol and around 80% fat content. Shop around! See what you can find!

From an average sample of a few brands the below fat percentages were calculated as a rough guide.

Food	Serving size	Calories	Fat %
Dark chocolate (85% cocoa solids)	½ oz. (14g)	89	74%
Dark chocolate (80% cocoa solids)	½ oz. (14g)	84	72%
Dark chocolate (75% cocoa solids)	½ oz. (14g)	82	66%
Cocoa powder (unsweetened)	1 oz. (28g)	75	50%

FRUIT AND VEGETABLES

This list includes an assortment of **Vegetables** that offer plenty of volume and texture to feedings and a couple of **Fruits** as well. Feel free to add something from this healthy selection to bulk up a meal. As you can see from the chart, for most vegetables it takes a lot to add significantly to the calories.

The main consideration you'll have while on a Fat Fast is that even though the vegetables and fruits listed are low GI, there is basically no fat going on in this list (with the notable exception of the avocado).

I wouldn't overthink it too much though – you'd have to eat a pretty big serving of vegetables to shift you out of Ketosis, and on a Fat Fast you can pretty easily keep track of how much is **too** much if you start to come close.

For example, combining a 16 calorie cup (70g) of mushrooms with a creamy soup mixture, the calories will be coming primarily from that delicious cream, not so much the mushrooms. And depending on variety, around half of those mushroom calories are protein, even better!

There's no argument about the nutrients that can be found in vegetables. Whether you fancy a potent dose of Vitamin A or K from some Spinach, or a boost of Vitamin C from Bell Peppers, if you can fit them into your non-fat caloric count during the Fast, I support you all the way.

Definitely **do** track your consumption of the easy to munch, mid GI stuff like berries. Non-fat calories like these, eaten by the handful can add up quickly.

Fat Fasting For Weight Loss Including 50 Low Carb & High Fat Recipes

Food	Serving size	Calories
Artichoke	1 medium heart (128g)	60
Arugula	½ cup (10g)	5
Asparagus	1 medium spear (16g)	3
Bell Peppers	1 cup (92g)	29
Blackberries	½ cup (72g)	31
Blueberries	½ cup (74g)	42
Bok Choy	½ cup (35g)	4
Broccoli	1 cup (91g)	31
Cabbage (chopped)	1 cup (89g)	22
Cauliflower (chopped)	1 cup (107g)	27
Celery	1 medium stalk	6
Cherry Tomatoes	1 cup (150g)	27
Cucumber (slices)	½ cup (52g)	8
Eggplant (cubed)	1 cup (82g)	20
Garlic	1 clove	5
Green Beans	1 cup (100g)	31
Jalapeno Peppers (sliced)	1 cup (90g)	26
Tomatoes (red, chopped)	1 cup (180g)	32
Lemon	1 fruit (84g)	24
Lettuce (shredded)	½ cup (18g)	3

Lime	1 fruit (67g)	20
Mushrooms (pieces)	1 cup (70g)	16
Peas	½ cup (49g)	20
Raspberries	½ cup (62g)	32
Spinach	½ cup (15g)	4
Strawberries	½ cup (72g)	24
Watercress	½ cup (17g)	2
Zucchini	1 cup (113g)	19

AVOCADOS

Avocados I'm going to put here in its own little section.

An avocado is rich in potassium, full of anti-inflammatory carotenoids, silky and smooth, and wonderful either just by itself with some salt, blended into a smoothie, chopped up in a salad or used in many other ways while cooking. I even use avocado in my Brownie recipe in Keto Living 3.

Food	Serving size	Calories	Fat %
Avocado (cubed)	½ cup (75g)	120	84%

FOODS TO ADD VOLUME

Two excellent options for adding volume to a feeding are **Shirataki Noodles** and **Stock (or Broth)**.

Shirataki Noodles are made from the root of a plant known as *konjac* which comes packed in a liquid that has a noticeable fishy odor.

Be aware that some versions include tofu which does give the noodles a better, more pasta like texture, however the added tofu increases the calories and adds some carbs to a serve.

There's not really any need to get the tofu noodle version though if you follow all of the below.

To get noodles ready for a dish in a way that improves texture, and tames their aroma, first drain and rinse the noodles well in a colander, then drop them in a pot of salted boiling water. Allow them to simmer for no longer than 3 minutes, then drain once more. They are for the most part ready to use at this point, so if you are lacking in patience you can skip the next bit and charge ahead with your recipe here.

Still here? Good. There is not as much need to do the next step if you have tofu shirataki noodles but regardless of which you have, I still think it helps.

After boiling them, transfer the noodles to a dry non-stick pan and heat them over a medium heat for several more minutes until they look dry and fishy liquid free. This extra effort will get you an even better texture, and then you can add them to your recipe with newfound amazing results.

Stock or Broth is a clever way to add volume to a recipe. Stock is mostly water, and many brands contain a good amount of sodium. For the most part they can be included in a recipe with only a small change to calories or percentage of fat.

Food	Serving size	Calories
Shirataki noodles	4 oz. (112g)	0
Shirataki tofu noodles	4 oz. (112g)	20
Stock	1 cup (240g)	38

OTHER FOODS WORTHY OF A MENTION

For that pop-in-your-mouth chip like crunch that is full of wonderful fat, you have to agree that **Pork Rinds** are an excellent creation!

They are also easily used as crumbing when ground fine. Be careful to check the fat to protein ratio on the product you purchase, some brands are better suited to a Fat Fast than others.

Also, I mentioned the hidden benefits of **Gelatin** earlier in the book, so don't forget about this. A flavored sugar free gelatin is great to have sitting in the fridge at the end of a Fat Fast day for that extra burst of late night munching.

For a superb and versatile, low-carb and low calorie, nutty alternative to regular milk get yourself some **Unsweetened Almond Milk**. It's around 70% fat, replaces cup for cup in baking, and is used in many of my recipes.

FLAVORS, SEASONINGS AND MORE

High fat foods are delicious and satisfying, but they can be even better with a dash of the right seasoning. Avoiding condiments and sauces that contain sugars or thickeners is important, but you can count on the following options to add a boost of flavor to your Fat Fast foods.

Citrus Zest can be added to cream cheese and nut butters, as well as a flavoring for the water you are drinking (you are drinking lots of water, right?).

Lemon juice is also great for blunting insulin. A squirt in a glass of water not only enhances the flavor but also helps with lowering your blood sugar response. Good to know, and worth experimenting with even after your Fat Fast ends!

Fresh Herbs and Spices are a staple of any kitchen, regardless of the diet you are on.

"Parsley, sage, rosemary and thyme", crooned Simon and Garfunkel in the 60's, as a nod to the virtues associated with certain herbs during medieval times.

Spices and herbs are notable for their well-documented health benefits and many international and ethnic dishes simply aren't authentic without the right pinch of this or that.

Herbs are also great in low calorie infused teas, many of which have antioxidant properties.

Look at a few recipes you are thinking of making and pick up any herbs and spices you are missing from the recipe and perhaps a couple of extras each time you head out. You'll soon be well stocked, and your kitchen creations will only benefit by expanding the selection on your shelf.

Additional Ingredients such as baking soda, baking powder, various essences, and some thickeners such as xanthan gum are always good to keep nearby, when changing the consistency or flavor of a dish is needed.

Sauces and pastes are plentiful and there are many excellent low-carb options. Mix up an exotic sauce of your own, or experiment with a dash of soy, a splash of Tobasco, some spicy salsa. A red curry, pesto or a dollop of mustard can really elevate a dish. Oh, and don't forget to stock some vinegar, and perhaps keep a bottle of red and white "cooking" wine nearby.

The applications for zest, herbs, spices, essences and sauces cannot be overstated enough – a boring dish can become an exotic journey with just a sprinkle of the right spice. Combine a little mint sauce with some lamb, and suddenly you have a side order of nostalgia with your meal.

It's that extra little layer that can bring everything together. Anyone who has ever completed a Fat Fast while chewing on the side of a block of cream cheese has forgotten the magic of cooking, and how a little seasoning and creativity can truly elevate a dish.

ANYTHING SWEET?

The right **Sugar Substitutes** are fantastic.

Before I continue into the section on sweeteners, allow me to digress for a moment to glowingly appraise our Ketogenic lifestyle.

There are recipes to whip up scrumptious low-carb bread substitutes with ease if we want to make a burger. We have ways to make pizza bases with almond flour and cheese or cauliflower that taste fantastic when topped with pepperoni and mushrooms.

And with the right sugar substitute we can make muffins, brownies, ice cream, sweet coffees and more that taste amazing.

So where exactly is the restriction on Keto? I tell you the only time it's ever a pain for me is when I'm walking through the snack food section before seeing a movie.

These days I just make sure I have some nuts and a diet drink on hand. Pork rinds are good too, but they can be loud and crunchy in a cinema!

My point is, that with a little effort, this diet is maintainable, and with some kitchen skills, as close as you get to not even being on a diet at all. Thankfully, I don't like potatoes. Or I might miss hot chips. Potato chips are easy enough to substitute.

Anyway, let's talk sweet stuff.

Sugar substitutes have been covered in much greater detail in the 2nd Keto Living Cookbook, 'Keto Living 2: Lose Weight with 101 Yummy & low-carb Ketogenic Savory and Sweet Snacks'.

A bit I have never mentioned before is the two major concerns low-carb dieters have with sweeteners.

First – that sweeteners can feed the addiction to sugar. I'm not sure I buy in to this. A great deal of the desire to eat more sugar goes far beyond the taste on the tongue, but the reaction to the carbohydrates that takes place in your body including the insulin response.

Many sweeteners, as well as being super low in caloric value, have practically no insulinogenic response either.

Sometimes I feel like a piece of low-carb sweetened cake?

If that makes me feel like more cake at a later date, I'll just eat **another low-carb slice**. I'm definitely not going to head off to the shop to buy a carb laden version. That ship has sailed.

The second thing people tend to parrot is that your body has an insulin response at the very *thought* of eating something that remotely resembles something sweet.

There is actually some science and anecdotal information supporting this, but to be clear, the response on a Ketogenic diet reported by many who test regularly is that there is either no change to insulin levels, or only a negligible change.

And in fact extensive studies[20] in 2010 on volunteers using sucralose and stevia determined that there is no consistent evidence that low calorie sweeteners cause any insulin release when ingested.

Also, some of the anecdotal information filtered down to us is mixed with misinformation.

Many people don't realize that a lot of main brands of sweetener are mixed with dextrose or maltodextrin which will with certainty achieve an insulin response, as the glycemic index of the filler in these sugar substitutes (GI – 100 and 110 respectively) are on a par with, or even higher than glucose (GI - 100).

Even some stevia products have been mixed with high glycemic fillers.

It's entirely reasonable, don't you think, that at least **some** of the reports of an insulin response are coming from people that **assume** their choice of sweetener is low GI, not realizing it's **full** of high GI fillers.

So my suggestion is to stick with the low GI, low Calorie sweeteners such as erythritol (GI – 1), pure stevia (GI – 0) and others like sucralose (GI – 0), and my cooking blend that I discuss in greater detail in Keto Living 2.

Measure your Ketogenic state yourself using tools discussed earlier in the book, and make your own mind up on whether eating sweeteners affects you in a way that stalls your progress. Everyone is different.

To me, the main concern regarding sweeteners is that excess consumption of some types can cause a bit of a stomach upset, but even that usually takes someone with a sensitive disposition and more than a couple of serves to achieve.

Also some sweeteners do bad things to rats, and some do not so it's important to be aware of which sweeteners make for a good choice.

That's my 2 cents. Now let's go over some more information on sweeteners.

Apologies to anyone who has read this next bit before. It's required reading, so I've included the below section on sweeteners in the front of all of my books (with the exception of a much lengthier exploration into sweeteners in Keto Living 2).

Here we go.

In cases where a recipe calls for a **granulated or powdered sugar substitute**, we are looking to use a product that is for all intents and purposes a cup for cup exchange of product by volume, using a granular blend for granular, and powdered for powdered.

In all nutritional panels this has been calculated and added to the totals as if the increasingly popular sweet polyol (or sugar alcohol), Erythritol was used, and this has been calculated at 0.2 carb calories per gram.

Erythritol, when used in direct replacement for sugar is 70% as sweet as sugar and a very nice low carb, low GI ingredient to use that is also dental friendly with minimal complaints of stomach upset at consumption levels of under 50g of product per day.

If the 70% sweetness doesn't quite meet the grade, a couple more tablespoons (per cup) can make it up without altering the structure of most recipes, or better still, blending in a couple of drops of a liquid sweetener of your choice such as Stevia or Sucralose can add a nice synergy to the flavor.

You'll want to avoid granular sugar substitutes that include Maltodextrin or Dextrose as a filler, as the GI and caloric content is actually very similar to sugar. Also avoid falling for packaging claims of zero calories that may not be telling the whole story.

Now, in the case a recipe calls for a **liquid sugar substitute**, I have kept things simple, and simply recommended liquid Stevia.

With liquid Stevia, sweetness intensity can vary from brand to brand depending on the actual percentage of steviol content added to the product (purer is better).

Without getting too technical, there is also variety in taste and bitterness of Stevia depending on whether the steviol extracted from the plant is Stevioside or the less bitter, and 50% sweeter Rebaudioside A (which I prefer), and this isn't always marked clearly on the label.

Also, if you choose something else like Sucralose as your preferred liquid sweetener, you'll need to adjust the quantity used, as the sweetness of Sucralose is about double that of Stevia.

Aside from the above, feel free to experiment with the many options out there as different substitutes yield different results in the final product, in more ways than one.

There is more information to be found in Keto Living 2 on this subject, but for now, this will help you enjoy creating the recipes contained within this book.

And remember, when it comes to sweetness, if in doubt, a taste test is usually the best practice!

HOW IMPORTANT IS IT TO EAT FIBER?

Fiber, fiber, fiber...

When I started writing this I hesitated on how to proceed, because fiber has come under some scrutiny lately as being less the golden goose everyone thought it to be. Nothing is ever easy is it?

The easy path most authors take, and the popular belief is that fiber reduces blood sugar, boosts health, improves digestion, cleans up blood lipids, and relieves constipation, however there is also some studies[21] focusing on the potential negative attributes of fiber.

So which is it? Is fiber devoid of nutrition and abrasive on the intestines? Is it cause for bloating and other maladies? On the other hand, is fiber a beneficial and essential prebiotic? And does it or doesn't it help with better BM's? There are arguments in both columns, and the debate is heating up.

When getting bogged down in conflicting research it's sometimes better to pause and consider a cautious approach. For example, attempting to completely remove fiber from a diet would therefore cause an individual to stop eating nutritious leafy or cruciferous vegetables which subsequently removes the benefits of these as well.

Sigh... It seems that periodically this happens with everything we put in our bodies. There is always opposing viewpoints.

Anyhow, let me be clear on my stance. This is **not** a platform for me to say to avoid fiber. I'm just suggesting that fastidiously counting how many fiber grams you should or should not consume, and looking to fiber as a digestive cure-all is potentially less black and white than we've been told, and at the very least I would encourage individuals to do further research exploring this topic.

But, as I digress often and this is not a book about fiber or digestive issues.

It's a book about a short term low calorie, fat biased diet. And the good news is that eating sufficient fats usually gets things moving downstairs anyway.

In relation *specifically* to a Fat Fast, here's what we need to know.

When working out our macronutrient calculations, remember that fiber isn't counted as having any caloric worth, and on labels, needs to be **deducted** from a **US Nutritional Panel** carbohydrate count.

For example, if we chow down 100 grams of raspberries (nom, nom, nom), and this is listed as having 12 grams of carbohydrates with 6 of those being fiber, we can smile to ourselves knowing that this delicious feast of low glycemic anti-oxidant berries had only half the carb induced guilt.

However, be aware that different countries list fiber on nutritional panels differently. Where in the US we calculate a Net carb figure by deducting fiber grams from carbohydrate grams on a label, in Australia, the UK and Europe for instance, fiber grams have **already** been deducted, so Net carbohydrates are what is already shown under Carbohydrates on the nutritional panel.

Also, fiber can help bulk up a meal into a more satiating feed, as it has substance but no usable calories. Mixing in some shirataki noodles is a great example of adding bulk to a meal from fiber without adding calories, and being able to eat a meal in quantity without calorie concerns has a nice psychological effect, especially while on a Fat Fast.

Fiber may also help you to feel full as it slows digestion, which is beneficial on a Fat Fast, and on an everyday Ketogenic diet it can help with flattening blood sugar spikes when eaten alongside higher glycemic foods.

In day to day life, when it comes to fiber I'm reasonably neutral. I don't avoid it and I don't deliberately fill up on it. I just make sure it's measured appropriately in calculating Net carbs, which to me, remains the most important figure in Keto.

However, sorry to do this, but to throw in one last curve ball, fiber *can* cause some water retention which can of course skew the results on the scale.

If you really want to be a stickler about seeing the best numbers, maybe allow more fiber on the first day or two of a Fat Fast to help you bridge any little hunger cravings and then, as the body adjusts, ease off on the fiber on the last day or two to maximize what you see on the scale. Phew! Follow all that?

WHAT CAN I DRINK?

Lots of water! For many reasons.

Ahhh... refreshing water, would madam or monsieur like it room temperature? Or may I suggest chilled? Or... ooh la la! Heaven forbid – sparkling?

Seriously though. Drink water. Preferably filtered or purified if you can.

Water is zero calories, and easily made more appealing or flavored by adding some fresh lemon juice (which is insulin blunting), or a crushed herb sprig.

I personally own a SodaStream and some diet Stevia and Sucralose flavors so I fizz mine up and flavor it that way. Any way you get it, water is good stuff.

Drink eight, 10-12 oz. (280-340ml) glasses a day. Studies show that without sufficient water the kidneys share the workload with the liver reducing the liver's ability to complete its other jobs, one of which is metabolizing fat.

Also if you don't drink enough water, the body actually retains water for later. So come on, let's get some flow happening, you're not a camel!

Drink enough and fluid retention isn't anywhere near as much of a problem. If you are overweight, you'll need to drink even more to combat this, around another glass for every 20-30 lbs you are overweight.

Water also helps with maintaining muscle tone, and flushing waste. It cushions joints, protects organs, and keeps our body temperature regulated.

You can even speed up weight loss by drinking really cold water to make your body work metabolically while it works to warm you up.

The only real warning with water consumption is in extreme quantities, you can actually drink too much. You need a **lot** though.

Below 4 quarts (a gallon), will for most people be fine. Just remember that too much water, such as 2-3 gallons *can* actually be dangerous.

Don't overthink it - work out how many glasses of water you need to meet your guidelines and stay hydrated.

Most of us are lucky enough to have water in abundance, and it contributes nicely to weight losses. There's really no excuse to avoid topping up your glass throughout the day.

OTHER NON-CALORIC BEVERAGES

You can enjoy basically any non-caloric beverage you like. I'm personally a fan of **Diet Soda and Squash**. These artificially sweetened drinks contain a lot of water and therefore count towards water consumption.

I'm not, however a proponent of the sweetener Aspartame. The jury keeps leaving the room on the overall safety of this one, and for the quantity of soda I drink, it becomes a consideration.

Stevia based diet drinks are great if you can find them, otherwise you can make your own with a SodaStream[22] and one of the Stevia or Sucralose flavors, exactly the way you like to make it.

Diet drinks in general get a bad rap. We've all heard that heavy consumers of diet sodas are opening themselves to a myriad of future drama such as... (deep breath)... declining kidney function, increased risk of metabolic syndrome, obesity, mitochondria issues, hives, asthma, irritations to skin, eyes, and mucous membrane, and dissolving tooth enamel from the acid.

I believe that correlation does not equal causation. When you study a group of people drinking diet soda, many with metabolic syndrome is the cause of their medical problems from the diet soda? Or... did a lifetime of poor dietary choices prompt them to drink diet soda in the first place?

Again, do your own research. I believe that much of what is claimed is a myth.

There is no study I can find that unwaveringly confirms the most popular claims of long-term health risk from drinking diet drinks, with the exception of a couple of things.

Try and stick to the recommended sweeteners. And remember to brush your teeth, sodas are acidic.

To quantify this, water has a neutral pH of 7. Battery acid has a pH of 1. Most sodas including diet, sit around 3.

Particularly the acid to watch is phosphoric acids, found in many branded drinks and can affect enamel. Phosphoric acid is also loosely linked to kidney stone formation although again, this has been debated.

To be safest, I simply mix my own diet sodas at home with a SodaStream to control the pH impact. Carbonic acid itself seems to have a negligible effect on enamel, there are also flavors that don't contain phosphoric acids.

Can you tell I kind of love my SodaStream? ☺

If pH levels genuinely are a concern to you, you can get test strips online.

Ultimately, a Fat Fast is only for a few days or so – if you have any concerns about any of this and really want to be strict during this time, then lemon water or herbal teas will give you an easy time of it!

What about alcohol?

During the Fat Fast, you'll need to avoid alcohol.

Alcohol on a regular Ketogenic diet has its place if low GI, low carbohydrate options are adhered to in sensible quantities, and as long as you are aware that alcohol puts the benefits of Ketosis on hold while it is processed out of your system ahead of every other macronutrient. Oh, and you may already know that the effects of alcohol seem to hit harder and faster when on Keto, so there's some caution to consider there too.

On the Fat Fast, you'll just not be able to maintain 1000 calories at 90% fat while drinking alcohol.

Even low-carbohydrate beers and wines have more calories than you can afford while on a Fat Fast.

I mean feel free to prove me wrong! I'm sure somebody out there can think of a small cream based drink... Let me think... Maybe a half shot of rum or so, some coconut milk, a little pineapple flavouring, some crushed ice... Now sing, "If you like pina coladaaaaaaassss, and gettin' caught in the rain..."

My recommendation? I wouldn't make that drink as it would use up ¼ of my calories for the day, and also for reasons discussed above. Would it actually work though?

Hmmm... Be right back. Doing science stuff.

SHOULD I TAKE ANY SUPPLEMENTS?

Whenever you fast, you are restricting calories, so of course, the quantity of nutrients will drop.

As far as a Fat Fast is concerned (and in fact also outside of a Fat Fast), I suggest you should at least be taking a nice potent multi-vitamin supplement each day, and keep up daily potassium (1g), sodium (2g) and magnesium (300mg) levels as discussed earlier in the section on diet safety.

Two other supplements to consider taking are fish oil (or krill oil), and also I'd recommend you find out your Vitamin D levels and get this back on track with appropriate supplementation.

There may be other supplements you'd like to consider, such as citrates for your kidneys. Your choices will ultimately depend upon your individual circumstances and research, making sure that you avoid anything that contraindicates with anything else you are taking.

Nutritional and dietary supplementation should always take into account your overall health goals and concerns, and if you need additional advice, I suggest you have a consultation with someone qualified to evaluate your specific needs and come up with an appropriate plan.

Now, let's get into some recipes!

SAVORY SNACKS

CUCUMBER, SMOKED SALMON AND AVOCADO ROUNDS

Smoked salmon and avocado make an enticing combination. Top with the cucumber slices just before eating. The salmon mixture and the egg will keep in the fridge until the next day if tightly wrapped in cling film.

Makes 10

INGREDIENTS:

½ a cucumber, cut into 10 x ¼ inch (0.6cm) slices

4 ounces (113g) full fat cream cheese

3 tbsp. sour cream

1 tsp. olive oil

1 small, ripe avocado

1 tsp. lemon juice, freshly squeezed

2 ounces (57g) fresh salmon, cooked and finely flaked

1 fresh egg, hard boiled, peeled and chopped

Salt and pepper (to taste)

Powdered cayenne pepper (to garnish)

DIRECTIONS:

1. Remove the avocado flesh from the skin and discard the pip.
2. Mash the avocado together with the cream cheese, olive oil and sour cream and beat well until smooth.
3. Stir in the flaked salmon.
4. Season to taste with the lemon juice, salt and pepper.
5. Spoon, the mixture evenly onto the cucumber slices.
6. Sprinkle with cayenne pepper and some chopped hardboiled egg.
7. Serve and enjoy.

Nutritional Facts per round: Calories 109, Fat 9.9g, Carbohydrate 2.8g, Dietary Fiber 1.4g, **Net Carbs 1.4g***, Protein 3.1g,* **Calories from Fat 83%**

CHILI, BACON CHEESE BALLS

These little, pop-in-your-mouth savory cheese balls pack a spicy punch.

Makes 6

INGREDIENTS:

4 ounces (113g) full fat cream cheese

1½ ounces (43g) strong Cheddar cheese, shredded

3 x 1 ounce (28g) slices of bacon

1 jalapeno pepper

1 tbsp. fresh parsley, finely chopped

Few drops of fresh lemon juice

Olive oil (for frying)

Salt and pepper (to taste)

DIRECTIONS:

1. Fry or broil the bacon until crispy and set aside to cool.

2. When cool, chop the bacon very finely and set aside.

3. Seed and finely chop the Jalapeno pepper and add it to the bacon.

4. Beat together the cream cheese and the shredded Cheddar until well blended.

5. Beat in the lemon juice and some seasoning to taste.

6. Add the parsley, bacon and pepper and mix everything very well together.

7. Divide the mixture into 6 even sized portions.

8. Roll each portion into a ball and place them on a parchment lined plate.

9. Refrigerate for a couple of hours for the flavors to develop.

*Nutritional Facts per ball: Calories 167, Fat 15.9g, Carbohydrate 1.0g, Dietary Fiber 0g, **Net Carbs 1.0g**, Protein 5.0g, **Calories from Fat 85%***

AVOCADO AND BACON MINGLE

Avocado and bacon is a wonderful flavor match. Eat up within the same day or seal and refrigerate overnight for breakfast the next day.

Serves 4

INGREDIENTS:

1 small avocado

2 x 1 ounce (28g) slices of bacon

2 garlic cloves, crushed

4 drops Tabasco sauce

½ tsp. fresh lemon juice

½ cup (116g) full fat cream cheese

Olive oil (for frying)

Salt and pepper (to taste)

DIRECTIONS:

1. Fry the bacon slices in a small skillet over a medium high heat.
2. When the bacon is crisp, remove from the heat and set aside.
3. Halve, stone and peel the avocado.
4. Cut the avocado flesh into chunks.
5. Beat the cream cheese, Tabasco sauce and lemon juice.
6. Beat in the crushed garlic.
7. Finely chop the bacon and stir it into the cheese mixture.
8. Carefully mix together the cheese mixture and the chopped avocado and serve.

Nutritional Facts per serve: Calories 243, Fat 23.7g, Carbohydrate 4.3g, Dietary Fiber 2.3g, **Net Carbs 2.0g,** *Protein 4.7g,* **Calories from Fat 88%**

HERBY PUFFS

Cheesy egg puffs! Sprinkle different herbs of your choice into the mixture for a change in flavor. Add some butter for extra taste. Be sure to remember to keep a count of your calories.

Makes 6

INGREDIENTS:

8 ounces (227g) full fat cream cheese

2 large fresh eggs, separated

1 tbsp. Italian herb seasoning

Salt and pepper (to taste)

DIRECTIONS:

1. Pre-heat the oven to 375°F (191°C).
2. Line a 6 cup muffin pan with paper cases.
3. Beat the cream cheese in a bowl until soft and smooth.
4. Beat in the egg yolks into the cheese.
5. Season to taste.
6. Whisk the egg whites until stiff peaks form.
7. Fold into the cream cheese along with the Italian herbs.
8. Spoon equally among the muffin cups and place in the hot oven.
9. Bake for 15 – 20 minutes until risen and brown.
10. Serve warm.

*Nutritional Facts per puff: Calories 156, Fat 14.8g, Carbohydrate 1.1g, Dietary Fiber 0g, **Net Carbs 1.1g**, Protein 5.0g, **Calories from Fat 86%***

SMOKED MACKEREL PÂTÉ

Enjoy this tasty pâté on slices of cucumber or wrapped in crisp fresh lettuce. This recipe is easy to double depending on the amount you need. Keep it in the fridge for a couple of days only and if the mixture splits, beat it with a fork to bring it back to the original consistency.

Serves 4

INGREDIENTS:

4 ounces (113g) smoked mackerel, skinned and boned

4 ounces (113g) full fat cream cheese

2 tbsp. sour cream

1 tbsp. lemon juice, freshly squeezed

½ tsp. freshly ground black pepper

1 tbsp. chopped chives (to garnish)

Salt (to taste)

DIRECTIONS:

1. Place all of the ingredients except the chives into a processor or blender.

2. Pulse until light and smooth. Add a little water if the mixture is too thick.

3. Spoon into a serving bowl and enjoy.

Nutritional Facts per serve: Calories 193, Fat 17.6g, Carbohydrate 1.1g, Dietary Fiber 0.2g, **Net Carbs 0.9g**, *Protein 7.9g,* **Calories from Fat 82%**

CHEESY PORK PATTIES

Make sure that your purchased pork sausages are meaty, fatty sausages with without any starches or grains added – if you can't be sure then grind your own pork belly, adding a few spices as you go.

Makes 12

INGREDIENTS:

12 ounces (340g) pork sausage, 100% meat

4 ounces (113g) Cheddar cheese, shredded

1 medium fresh egg

1 small red chili, finely chopped

½ cup (35g) pork rinds (for coating), finely ground

Salt and pepper (to taste)

Coconut oil (for frying)

DIRECTIONS:

1. Remove the sausage meat from the skins and place in a large bowl. Or use your freshly ground meat.

2. Mix in the shredded cheese, egg, chili and seasoning and blend well.

3. Form into 12 patties of equal size with lightly dampened hands if the mixture sticks.

4. Lightly toss in the pork rind.

5. Heat the coconut oil in a deep skillet and fry the pork patties until brown on all sides and crisp.

6. Serve warm.

Nutritional Facts per patty: Calories 188, Fat 16.8g, Carbohydrate 0.2g, Dietary Fiber 0g, **Net Carbs 0.2g***, Protein 9.2g,* **Calories from Fat 81%**

PARMESAN CHICKEN BALLS

These tangy chicken bites are rolled in cilantro and green onion and melt in your mouth. With a fairly low calorie count, treat yourself to a couple.

Makes 12

INGREDIENTS:

3 ounces (85g) ground chicken breast meat, cooked in a little olive oil

1 ounce (28g) Parmesan cheese, grated

1 ounce (28g) Cheddar cheese, shredded

10 ounces (283g) full fat cream cheese

3 tbsp. sour cream

½ tsp. chili sauce

1 green onion, minced

2 tbsp. cilantro, finely chopped

Salt and pepper (to taste)

DIRECTIONS:

1. Beat the cream cheese and sour cream in a medium sized bowl until smooth.
2. Stir in the chicken, Parmesan, Cheddar, chili sauce and salt and pepper to taste.
3. On a plate, mix together the green onion and cilantro.
4. Divide the chicken mixture into 12 equal portions and drop them onto the herbs.
5. Carefully roll each in the herbs to form balls.
6. Place in the refrigerator to set.
7. Serve and enjoy. Keep any leftovers in the refrigerator and eat within 2 days.

Nutritional Facts chicken ball: Calories 124, Fat 11.4g, Carbohydrate 1.0g, Dietary Fiber 0g, **Net Carbs 1.0g**, *Protein 4.8g,* **Calories from Fat 82%**

PEPPERONI CHEESE BASKETS

Slices of pepperoni filled with a tangy mixture of cream cheese.

Makes 4

INGREDIENTS:

3 ounces (85g) pepperoni, sliced into 4

4 ounces (113g) full fat cream cheese

¼ cup (59ml) sour cream

2 cloves garlic, grated

1 ounce (28g) grated red bell pepper

Dash Tabasco sauce

Salt and pepper (to taste)

Shredded lettuce (to serve)

DIRECTIONS:

1. Beat together all of the ingredients, except the pepperoni and lettuce, until well combined.

2. Place a slice of pepperoni into each of 4 muffin cups which have been lined with cling film; flute the edges to make it fit if necessary.

3. Divide the cheese mixture equally among the cups.

4. Place in the refrigerator for an hour for the flavors to develop.

5. Remove the cups with the aid of the cling film lining and serve with some shredded lettuce.

*Nutritional Facts per cup: Calories 243, Fat 22.3g, Carbohydrate 3.1g, Dietary Fiber 0.5g, **Net Carbs 2.6g**, Protein 7.8g, **Calories from Fat 83%***

STUFFED JALAPENOS

These tangy little peppers with a cheese and bacon filling are a delicious pop-in-the-mouth snack for any time of the day. Allow yourself a couple of these easy to make treats!

Makes 6

INGREDIENTS:

6 Jalapeno peppers, seeded and sliced open

3 tbsp. cream cheese

3 tbsp. sour cream

1 tbsp. coconut oil

2 x 1 ounce (28g) slices of bacon, crisped and crumbled

1 tsp. hot chili sauce

Salt and pepper (to taste)

DIRECTIONS:

1.   Pre-heat the oven to 375°F (191°C).

2.   Line a small baking dish with parchment paper.

3.   Prepare the filling by beating together the cream cheese, sour cream, coconut oil, chili sauce and seasoning.

4.   Stir through the crumbled bacon.

5.   Using a teaspoon, fill the peppers with the cheese mixture.

6.   Place on the prepared dish and bake for 10 – 12 minutes until well heated through.

7.   Serve warm.

8.   These poppers do not keep well so eat them up and make some more!

Nutritional Facts per jalapeno: Calories 102, Fat 10.0g, Carbohydrate 1.6g, Dietary Fiber 0.6g, ***Net Carbs 1.0g****, Protein 2.0g,* ***Calories from Fat 88%***

SAVORY STUFFED EGGS

A traditional, all-time favorite, these little egg bites have a bit of spice to them!

Makes 8 halves

INGREDIENTS:

4 medium fresh eggs, hard boiled

1 slice bacon, crisped and crumbled

4 tbsp. full fat cream cheese

4 tbsp. sour cream

1½ tbsp. real mayonnaise

1 tsp. fresh red chili, finely chopped

Salt and freshly ground pepper (to taste)

Paprika or cayenne pepper (to garnish)

DIRECTIONS:

1. Peel the eggs and cut them in half lengthways.

2. Remove the yolks and place them in a small bowl. Place the whites on a plate.

3. Mash the yolks well with the back of a fork and beat them together with the cream cheese, sour cream and mayonnaise.

4. Beat in the chili and the bacon crumbles.

5. Season to taste.

6. Spoon the yolk mixture into reserved egg whites, evenly distributing it among them.

7. Sprinkle with paprika or cayenne and serve.

*Nutritional Facts per half: Calories 98, Fat 9.0g, Carbohydrate 0.7g, Dietary Fiber 0g, **Net Carbs 0.7g**, Protein 3.8g, **Calories from Fat 83%***

BACON BUNDLES

Nutritional information on these is based on using nice and fatty slices of bacon. The nuts, cream, and cheese fuse nicely with the meat for a taste sensation you won't forget.

Makes 6

INGREDIENTS:

6 x 1 ounce (28g) slices of bacon

3 ounces (85g) Cheddar cheese, cut into 12 sticks

1 tsp. hot chili sauce

1½ tbsp. full fat cream cheese

3 tbsp. macadamia nuts, finely chopped

DIRECTIONS:

1. Pre-heat the oven to 400°F (204°C).

2. Lay the bacon slices on a baking tray and bake until well browned but not crisp – about 15 minutes.

3. Remove from the oven.

4. Cool a little and then sprinkle with the chili sauce.

5. Sprinkle over the chopped nuts.

6. Place a stick of cheese on each bacon slice and roll up – like a sausage roll. Secure the ends with a tooth pick if necessary.

7. Put the bacon bundles back into the oven for 5 – 10 minutes or so to melt the cheese.

8. Remove from the oven and serve warm topped with a teaspoon of cream cheese.

Nutritional Facts per bundle: Calories 214, Fat 20.0g, Carbohydrate 1.2g, Dietary Fiber 0g, **Net Carbs 1.2g***, Protein 7.6g,* **Calories from Fat 84%**

BOLOGNA SAUSAGE AND CHEESE WRAPPED ASPARAGUS

Scrumptious, quick and just so simple! Halve the ingredients and number of serves if you are only making these for yourself.

Serves 8

INGREDIENTS:

8 ounces (227g) fresh asparagus, peeled and chopped into half inch (1.25cm) pieces

16 x ½ ounce (14g) slices of bologna sausage

4 ounces (113g) full fat cream cheese

2 ounces (57g) Cheddar cheese, finely shredded

1 tbsp. olive oil

DIRECTIONS:

1. Place 2 slices of the bologna together.

2. Repeat this for all 8 servings.

3. Divide the asparagus pieces among the portions.

4. Top the asparagus with some cream cheese and a sprinkling of Cheddar cheese.

5. Wrap the sides of the bologna over the top of the asparagus. Secure with toothpicks threaded through.

6. In a large skillet heat the olive oil and fry the wrapped asparagus for about 6 minutes turning carefully half way through.

7. Serve whilst still hot. Mind the toothpick!

Nutritional Facts per serve: Calories 182, Fat 16.3g Carbohydrate 2.6g, Dietary Fiber 0.6g, **Net Carbs 2.0g**, *Protein 6.5g,* **Calories from Fat 81%**

SMOKY BACON AND CHIVE CREAM

Savory fat bomb? Cheesy dip? Actually a bit of both.

Serves 8

INGREDIENTS:

3 x 1 ounce (28g) smoked bacon slices, crisped and crumbled

½ cup (116g) full fat cream cheese

1 cup (237ml) sour cream

2 tbsp. coconut butter, softened

½ tsp. freshly ground black pepper

2 tbsp. fresh chives, chopped

DIRECTIONS:

1. Beat together the cream cheese, sour cream and coconut butter.

2. Beat in the black pepper and chives.

3. Stir through the bacon.

4. Spoon into a clean bowl, cover with cling film and place in the refrigerator for an hour for the flavors to develop.

5. Serve.

Nutritional Facts per serve: Calories 192, Fat 18.9g, Carbohydrate 2.7g, Dietary Fiber 0.7g, **Net Carbs 2.0g**, *Protein 3.6g,* **Calories from Fat 89%**

SAVORY TUNA CREAM

This oily fish in a creamy sauce can be spiced up further by adding more Tabasco.

Serves 8

INGREDIENTS:

7 ounces (198g) canned tuna in oil

½ cup (118ml) sour cream

1 cup (237ml) heavy cream

½ cup (119ml) coconut cream

1 small lemon, juiced

4 drops Tabasco sauce (to taste)

2 anchovy fillets

2 tbsp. olive oil

Salt and pepper (to taste)

DIRECTIONS:

1. Flake the tuna into small pieces in a medium sized bowl and set aside.

2. Beat together the 3 different creams together with the lemon juice, olive oil and Tabasco.

3. Thoroughly mash the anchovies.

4. Add the anchovies and the cream mixture to the tuna.

5. Mix well. Season as necessary though you may find the anchovies already add enough salty flavors.

6. Place the tuna cream into a clean bowl, cover with cling wrap and refrigerate for an hour.

7. Serve as is or as a dip with strips of cucumber.

Nutritional Facts per serve: Calories 197, Fat 17.8g, Carbohydrate 2.5g, Dietary Fiber 0.5g, **Net Carbs 2.0g***, Protein 8.0g,* **Calories from Fat 81%**

BACON AND SAUSAGE FRITTATA

Bacon, pork sausage and Cheddar cheese combine in this versatile dish. It is worth making a full quantity to share, and also it keeps well in the refrigerator so can be eaten either warm or cold.

Serves 10

INGREDIENTS:

6 x 1 ounce (28g) slices of bacon

2 tbsp. olive oil

2 pork sausages, 100% meat

6 medium fresh eggs

1 cup (237ml) heavy cream

½ cup (118ml) sour cream

1 tsp. dijon mustard

1 tsp. onion powder

1½ cups (199g) Cheddar cheese, shredded

Salt and pepper (to season)

DIRECTIONS:

1. Preheat the oven to 375°F (191°C).

2. Using a skillet that can go into the oven, heat the olive oil over a medium high heat and sauté the bacon until crispy.

3. Set the bacon to one side and when cool snip into small pieces.

4. In the same skillet fry the pork sausages until cooked and brown. Remove and set aside to cool.

5. When cool cut into small cubes.

6. Beat together the eggs, creams, mustard, onion powder and seasoning.

7. Beat in one cup (133g) of shredded cheese.

8. Place the bacon and sausage back into the skillet.

9. Pour over the cheesy egg mixture.

10. Place back on the hot plate and cook gently for a few minutes, lifting the sides of the frittata to let some of the egg mixture go to the base of the skillet.

11. Sprinkle the reaming cheese on top.

12. When the egg mixture is nearly set put the skillet into the hot oven.

13. Cook for 10 – 15 minutes until fully set.

14. Remove and place under a hot broiler if liked to brown.

15. Cool a little and then serve.

*Nutritional Facts per serve: Calories 286, Fat 26.3g, Carbohydrate 1.7g, Dietary Fiber 0g, **Net Carbs 1.7g**, Protein 11.2g, **Calories from Fat 83%***

SAVORY MEALS

SMOKED SALMON BAKE

A tasty, warm lunchtime or dinner dish when you feel like something a little more substantial. Increase the quantities to make for others. A salad of sliced cucumber and crisp lettuce would accompany this nicely.

Serves 1

INGREDIENTS:

¼ tbsp. butter

1 medium fresh egg, separated

1½ ounce (43g) smoked salmon pieces, chopped

1 tbsp. chives, finely chopped

2 tbsp. sour cream

1 tbsp. coconut oil

Salt and pepper (to taste)

DIRECTIONS:

1. Pre-heat the oven to 375°F (191°C).

2. Lightly butter a 4 inch (10cm) ovenproof dish and set aside.

3. Finely chop the salmon.

4. Beat together the egg yolk, chives, coconut oil and sour cream until light and fluffy.

5. Gently fold in the smoked salmon and seasoning.

6. Whisk the egg white until it forms soft peaks.

7. Fold into the salmon mixture.

8. Pour or spoon into the prepared dish and bake in the hot oven for about 20 minutes until golden brown and firm to the touch.

9. Serve as soon as you remove the dish from the oven.

*Nutritional Facts per serve: Calories 308, Fat 27.7g, Carbohydrate 1.6g, Dietary Fiber 0g, **Net Carbs 1.6g**, Protein 14.2g, **Calories from Fat 81%***

CHEESE AND MUSHROOM SOUFFLE OMELET

This omelet has a creamy mushroom center and is easily tweaked with different fillings.

Serves 2

INGREDIENTS:

2 medium fresh eggs

1 tbsp. cold water

¼ cup (58g) full fat cream cheese

2 ounces (57g) mushrooms, chopped

1 tbsp. butter

1 tsp. fresh parsley, chopped finely

Salt and pepper (to taste)

Paprika or cayenne pepper (to garnish)

DIRECTIONS:

1. Heat half of the butter in a small skillet and sauté the mushrooms until tender.

2. Set aside to cool.

3. Beat the cream cheese adding the chopped parsley along with the cooled mushrooms. Season to taste.

4. Preheat a broiler to high.

5. Heat the rest of the butter in a small clean skillet

6. Break the eggs into as small bowl and whisk together with the water and some seasoning until fluffy.

7. Pour the egg mixture into the skillet and cook the omelet gently by lifting the sides and allowing the uncooked egg to go underneath.

8. When nearly set, place the omelet under the hot broiler where it will puff up and cook in the centre.

9. Remove from the broiler, slide out of the skillet onto a plate.

10. Spoon over the cream cheese mixture and garnish with paprika or cayenne.

11. Fold over if desired. Cut in half and serve.

12. Eat while still hot.

*Nutritional Facts per serve: Calories 221, Fat 20.3g, Carbohydrate 2.0g, Dietary Fiber 0g, **Net Carbs 2.0g**, Protein 8.7g, **Calories from Fat 83%***

HAM AND CHEESY EGGS

Ham and eggs with a chili twist. You can increase the fat percentage a little by removing the egg white from one or two of the eggs.

Serves 3

INGREDIENTS:

¼ cup (33g) Cheddar cheese, shredded

2 ounces (57g) ham, cooked and chopped

3 medium fresh eggs

3 tbsp. sour cream

2 tbsp. full fat cream cheese

4 tbsp. heavy cream

1 green onions, finely chopped

4 tsp. chili salsa (hot or mild)

Salt and pepper

1 tbsp. extra virgin olive oil

DIRECTIONS:

1. Pre-heat the oven to 350°F (177°C).
2. Place the ham at the base of 3 small ovenproof dishes.
3. Beat together the eggs, cream cheese, sour cream, heavy cream and seasoning.
4. Beat in the chili salsa and the green onion.
5. Pour over the ham in the dishes.
6. Sprinkle the top of each with the Cheddar cheese.
7. Bake in the oven until the cheese has melted and the mixture bubbly.
8. Serve warm sprinkled with extra virgin olive oil.

Nutritional Facts per serve: Calories 294, Fat 26.1g, Carbohydrate 3.3g, Dietary Fiber 0.6g, **Net Carbs 2.7g**, *Protein 12.5g,* **Calories from Fat 80%**

CREAM OF CAULIFLOWER AND GREEN ONION SOUP

Enjoyable for a lunchtime snack or in the evening when you want some warming comfort food. If you have a few calories left, sprinkle on a little grated Cheddar cheese or ground pork rinds.

Serves 3

INGREDIENTS:

4 green onions, finely chopped

1 tbsp. olive oil

8 ounces (227g) cauliflower

¼ cup (60ml) heavy cream

½ cup (119ml) coconut milk

¼ cup (59ml) sour cream

1 cup (237ml) vegetable stock

Salt and pepper (to taste)

DIRECTIONS:

1. Break up the cauliflower into small florets and steam it until it is tender.

2. Heat the olive oil in a medium sized sauce pan and lightly sauté the green onions.

3. Add the cauliflower and toss it in the oil and onions.

4. Pour in the vegetable stock and coconut milk and bring to the boil. Simmer for 10 minutes.

5. Remove the pan from the heat pour the cauliflower and onions, together with the liquid into a blender.

6. Blend until smooth.

7. Add the heavy cream and sour cream and blend until creamy and well mixed.

8. Pour back into the saucepan and heat very gently over a low heat. Do not let the soup boil.

9. Serve hot.

Nutritional Facts per serve: Calories 238, Fat 22.1g, Carbohydrate 9.6g, Dietary Fiber 3.7g, **Net Carbs 5.9g**, *Protein 3.9g,* **Calories from Fat 84%**

CRUSTLESS QUICHE

This is awesome to cook and keep in the fridge for an on the go meal. Just warm a portion gently in a microwave before serving. A serve of this is a little higher in calories for a Fat Fast meal, so be sure to keep track!

Serves 6

INGREDIENTS:

3 x 1 ounce (28g) slices of bacon, cooked until crisp

3 large fresh eggs

¾ cup (179ml) heavy cream

4 ounces (113g) full fat cream cheese

2 tbsp. macadamia nut oil

¼ cup (59ml) coconut cream

1 tbsp. fresh parsley, finely chopped

¾ cup (99g) Cheddar cheese, shredded

Salt and pepper (to taste)

1 tsp. butter to grease

DIRECTIONS:

1. Pre-heat the oven to 375°F (191°C).
2. Grease a quiche dish with the butter.
3. Chop the cooked bacon into small pieces and place on the base of the dish.
4. Beat together the eggs, cream cheese, creams, oil, seasoning and parsley.
5. Stir in the Cheddar cheese.
6. Spoon carefully over the bacon pieces and place the quiche dish on a baking tin.
7. Cook the quiche in the hot oven for 25 – 30 minutes until set.
8. Remove from the oven and cool a little before serving.

Nutritional Facts per serve: Calories 353, Fat 34.1g, Carbohydrate 2.3g, Dietary Fiber 0.3g, **Net Carbs 2.0g,** *Protein 10.5g,* **Calories from Fat 87%**

CREAMED SALMON WITH MUSHROOMS

This fresh salmon dish is exquisite served with a creamy curried mushroom topping. The calories per serve are on the higher side for a serving, so keep that in mind when calculating your daily allowances.

Serves 2

INGREDIENTS:

3 ounces (85g) fresh salmon fillets

½ cup (119ml) coconut cream

1 tbsp. sour cream

1 tbsp. butter

4 ounces (113g) fresh mushrooms, sliced

1 tsp. Thai red curry paste

Salt and pepper (to taste)

DIRECTIONS:

1. Preheat the oven to 350°F (177°C).

2. Season the salmon fillets and place them in a small oven proof dish.

3. Bake in the oven for about 15 minutes until cooked.

4. Meanwhile, melt the butter in a medium sized skillet and sauté the mushrooms until tender and nicely browned.

5. Stir in the curry paste and cook for a couple of minutes until fragrant.

6. Stir in the coconut cream and the sour cream.

7. Serve the mushrooms over the salmon fillets.

Nutritional Facts per serve: Calories 326, Fat 29.6g, Carbohydrate 7.0g, Dietary Fiber 2.3g, **Net Carbs 4.7g**, *Protein 12.1g,* **Calories from Fat 82%**

ZUCCHINI AND SOUR CREAM SALAD

A crunchy salad to enjoy. It does not keep well so plan to eat it in one day if you can. Add some Tabasco sauce if you like, for a tang.

Serves 2

INGREDIENTS:

7 ounces (198g) fresh zucchini, washed and sliced or chunked

2 cloves garlic, grated

½ cup (118ml) sour cream

2 tsp. olive oil

1 tbsp. parsley, finely chopped

Salt and pepper to season

DIRECTIONS:

1. Mix together all of the ingredients except the zucchini.

2. Cover and place in the refrigerator for 30 minutes for the flavors to develop.

3. Place the prepared zucchini into a serving dish.

4. Toss in the creamy dressing.

5. Serve.

Nutritional Facts per serve: Calories 184, Fat 16.9g, Carbohydrate 6.9g, Dietary Fiber 1.2g, **Net Carbs 5.7g**, *Protein 3.3g,* **Calories from Fat 83%**

MUSHROOMS WITH MACADAMIA NUT STUFFING

These stuffed and broiled mushrooms with a nutty filling and covered with melted cheese are so exquisite! The recipe is easy to double if you'd like to make extra for later in the day.

Makes 2

INGREDIENTS:

2 mushroom caps – 2 inches (5cm) in diameter

2 tbsp. sour cream

½ ounce (14g) macadamia nuts, finely chopped

1 tbsp. fresh parsley, chopped

1 cloves garlic, finely chopped

1 tbsp. coconut oil, melted

1 tbsp. Cheddar cheese, shredded

Salt and pepper (to taste)

DIRECTIONS:

1. Lay the mushroom cups on a small non-stick broiler pan – top side down.

2. Place the nuts, parsley, garlic, sour cream and oil in a small bowl and beat with a wooden spoon until a rough paste is formed.

3. Spoon the nut mixture between the mushroom caps and top each with the Cheddar cheese.

4. Place under a hot broiler for 6 – 8 minutes until cooked through and the cheese is bubbling.

5. Serve warm.

*Nutritional Facts per mushroom: Calories 156, Fat 15.9g, Carbohydrate 2.8g, Dietary Fiber 0.9g, **Net Carbs 1.9g**, Protein 2.6g, **Calories from Fat 92%***

PORK AND SOY NOODLES

Shirataki noodles topped with an enticing savory pork and soy sauce is sure to satisfy.

Serves 4

INGREDIENTS:

12 ounces (340g) shirataki noodles, rinsed in cold water

2 ounces (57g) pork fat, ground

2 ounces (57g) belly pork, ground

2 tbsp. soy sauce

1 tsp. rice wine vinegar

1 tbsp. sour cream

1 tsp. chili sauce (sugar free)

2 tbsp. macadamia nut butter

3 cloves garlic, crushed

1 tsp. green ginger, grated

1 tsp. sesame oil

1 green onion, finely chopped

Pepper (to taste)

DIRECTIONS:

1. Boil the noodles for 2 – 3 minutes in water. Drain.

2. Mix the ground pork and fat with the soy sauce and rice wine vinegar. Set aside.

3. Mix together the macadamia butter, sour cream and chili sauce.

4. Heat the sesame oil gently in a medium skillet, do not let it burn.

5. Stir fry the pork meat mixture until it loses its color.

6. Add the garlic and the ginger and stir-fry for a minute longer until fragrant.

7. Add the nut butter mixture and stir through the meat until well incorporated.

8. Stir through the green onion and toss with the drained noodles.

9. Heat together until warmed through.

10. Serve.

*Nutritional Facts per serve: Calories 279, Fat 27.8g, Carbs 17.0g, Dietary Fiber 14.6g, **Net Carbs 2.4g**, Protein 4.7g, **Calories from Fat 90%***

SHIRATAKI NOODLES WITH ARTICHOKE PESTO SAUCE

The shirataki noodles lap up the flavor of the pesto – a classic combination made Fat Fast friendly with the addition of some cream.

Serves 2

INGREDIENTS:

8 ounces (227g) shirataki noodles, drained and rinsed

2 tbsp. basil pesto

1 tbsp. olive oil

3 tbsp. full fat cream cheese

½ cup (118ml) heavy cream

½ tsp. dried chili flakes (to taste)

4 ounces (113g) canned artichoke hearts, drained

Salt and pepper (to taste)

DIRECTIONS:

1. Finely chop the artichoke hearts.

2. Beat together the cream cheese, heavy cream, olive oil and the basil pesto in a small sauce pan.

3. Add the seasoning and chili flakes as well as the chopped artichoke hearts.

4. Warm gently over a low heat to just below boiling point.

5. While the cream sauce is warming, heat the noodles through for 2 – 3 minutes in a pan of simmering water.

6. When ready to serve, drain the noodles and toss them with the creamy sauce.

7. Serve.

Nutritional Facts per serve: Calories 234, Fat 23.4g, Carbohydrate 13.3g, Dietary Fiber 10.2g, **Net Carbs 3.1g,** *Protein 2.4g,* **Calories from Fat 90%**

CAULIFLOWER WITH HAM AND CHEESE

Smooth cauliflower is elevated to mouth-watering heaven, smothered lavishly with a rich creamy, cheesy sauce, and guaranteed to please.

Serves 4

INGREDIENTS:

2 cups (128g) cauliflower, cooked

2 ounces (57g) cooked ham, chopped

¾ cup (99g) Cheddar cheese, shredded

1 medium fresh egg

1 cup (237ml) heavy cream

¼ cup (59ml) sour cream

2 tbsp. fresh parsley, chopped

Salt and pepper (to taste)

1½ tbsp. olive oil

DIRECTIONS:

1. Preheat the oven to 350°F (177°C).
2. Grease a 7 inch (18cm) casserole dish with the olive oil or use 4 x individual oven proof dishes.
3. Chop the cauliflower into smallish pieces – not too small!
4. Place in the prepared cookware.
5. Sprinkle over the chopped ham.
6. Beat together the egg, creams and the seasoning.
7. Stir in the parsley and the Cheddar cheese.
8. Spoon the cheese mixture over the cauliflower.
9. Place the casserole in the hot oven and bake for 10 minutes until brown on the top.
10. Remove from the oven and serve while hot.

*Nutritional Facts per serve: Calories 302, Fat 27.0g, Carbohydrate 5.1g, Dietary Fiber 1.5g, **Net Carbs 3.6g**, Protein 11.1g, **Calories from Fat 81%***

CREAMY MUSHROOM SOUP

The succulent meat of the mushroom pieces combines so well with the smooth cream and is the perfect comfort food on a cold day.

Serves 4

INGREDIENTS:

12 ounces (340g) fresh mushrooms, wiped and chopped

2 cloves garlic, grated

2 tbsp. olive oil

1 tbsp. butter

1¼ pints (591ml) vegetable stock

1 bay leaf

1 sprig fresh parsley

1 sprig fresh thyme

1 cup (237ml) heavy cream, at room temperature

Salt and pepper to season

4 tbsp. sour cream to serve

DIRECTIONS:

1. Heat the olive oil and butter together in a large saucepan over a medium high heat.

2. When hot add the mushrooms. Sauté until brown.

3. Stir in the garlic and cook for another 20 seconds.

4. Pour in the vegetable stock. Add the fresh herbs.

5. Bring to the boil, turn down to a simmer and simmer for 30 minutes.

6. Remove the soup from the heat and cool a little before liquidising until smooth.

7. Return the soup to the saucepan and stir in the cream.

8. Warm through thoroughly but do not let the soup boil.

9. Serve hot in 4 soup bowls, topping each with a tablespoon of sour cream.

Nutritional Facts per serve: Calories 244, Fat 23.9g, Carbohydrate 6.0g, Dietary Fiber 1.6g, **Net Carbs 4.4g**, *Protein 4.4g,* **Calories from Fat 87%**

PORK SAUSAGE WITH MUSHROOMS AND SPINACH

Succulent and creamy mushrooms over pork sausage balls and topped with spinach make this Fat Fast dish a real treat. The calories are a little above average for the usual Fat Fast serving size, so remember to note this in your calculations.

Serves 4

INGREDIENTS:

4 ounces (113g) pork sausage meat, 100% ground meat

1 tbsp. olive oil

2 cloves garlic, minced

5 ounces (142g) baby spinach, washed

8 ounces (227g) mushrooms, sliced

½ cup (116g) full fat cream cheese

1 cup (237ml) heavy cream

1 tsp. lemon juice, freshly squeezed

Salt and pepper (to taste)

DIRECTIONS:

1. Mix the garlic into the sausage meat and season lightly.
2. With damp hands, roll the meat into 8 small balls.
3. Heat the oil in a medium sized skillet over a medium high heat.
4. Sauté the sausage balls until brown and cooked.
5. Remove the balls and keep warm.
6. In the same skillet sauté the mushrooms until brown.
7. Add the heavy cream and the cheese to the mushrooms and stir well together.
8. Add the sausage balls and add the lemon juice.
9. Heat through thoroughly but do not boil.
10. Place a separate skillet over a medium high heat and quickly wilt the baby spinach for 30 seconds.
11. Serve the creamy mushrooms and sausage balls and top each serving with an equal portion of spinach.

Nutritional Facts per serve: Calories 344, Fat 32.5g, Carbohydrate 5.3g, Dietary Fiber 1.4g, **Net Carbs 3.9g**, *Protein 10.0g,* **Calories from Fat 85%**

CREAMY SHRIMP SALAD

This refreshing shrimp salad is perfect served with crisp lettuce and cucumber slices.

Serves 6

INGREDIENTS:

6 ounces (170g) raw shrimp

3 tbsp. butter

1 clove garlic, grated

3 green onions, finely chopped

1 red chili pepper, seeded and chopped

1 cup (237ml) heavy cream

2 tbsp. coconut butter, softened

1 tsp. sun dried tomato paste

1 tsp. powdered paprika

Salt and pepper (to taste)

DIRECTIONS:

1. Clean and peel the shrimp.

2. Heat the butter in a medium skillet over a medium high heat.

3. Sauté the shrimp together with the garlic, onions and chili until pink and cooked through.

4. Remove from the heat and place in a bowl together with all of the juices. Leave to cool.

5. Beat together the cream, softened coconut butter, tomato paste and paprika. Season to taste.

6. When the shrimp is cool, stir through the cream.

7. Serve in individual glass bowls.

Nutritional Facts per serve: Calories 191, Fat 17.2g, Carbohydrate 2.6g, Dietary Fiber 1.2g, **Net Carbs 1.4g***, Protein 6.5g,* **Calories from Fat 81%**

CREAM CHEESE AND CUCUMBER GELATIN MOLD

A Fat Fast gelatin mold to set in the refrigerator and portion out as required. Serve with some extra cucumber slices if you like.

Serves 8

INGREDIENTS:

3 tsp. unflavored sugar free gelatin

1 tbsp. cold water

¼ pint (118ml) hot water

2 tbsp. lemon juice, freshly squeezed

16 ounces (454g) full fat cream cheese

7 ounces (198g) sour cream

½ medium cucumber, chopped, and seeded

Salt and pepper to season

DIRECTIONS:

1. Soak the gelatin in the cold water.

2. Add the soaked gelatin to the hot water and dissolve.

3. Add the lemon juice and a little salt. Set aside to cool.

4. Beat the cream cheese and the sour cream well together and season to taste.

5. Stir in the cooled gelatin mixture and the cucumber.

6. Rinse out a ring mold or a basin with cold water.

7. Pour in the creamy mixture and cover with cling film.

8. Place in the refrigerator to set for a couple of hours or overnight.

9. Unmold and serve.

Nutritional Facts per serve: Calories 259, Fat 25.0g, Carbohydrate 3.3g, Dietary Fiber 0.1g, **Net Carbs 3.2g**, *Protein 5.6g,* **Calories from Fat 87%**

SWEET SURPRISE

CHOCOLATE CREAM MOUSSE

Who would have thought that Fat Fasts can be full of silky chocolate, so creamy and smooth. Eat one now and keep the others in the refrigerator for the next day covered in cling film.

Serves 4

INGREDIENTS:

1 ounce (28g) dark chocolate (80% cocoa)

½ cup (118ml) heavy cream

3 tbsp. crème fraiche

3 tbsp. full fat cream cheese

1 extra-large fresh egg, white only

6 drops liquid stevia extract (adjust to taste)

DIRECTIONS:

1. Place the chocolate in a ceramic bowl over a pan of simmering water.

2. Melt and set aside to cool.

3. Beat the crème fraiche and the cream cheese together with the cooled chocolate.

4. Whisk the egg white until it forms soft peaks. Whisk in the liquid sweetener.

5. Using the whisk, fold the egg white into the chocolate mix.

6. When it is nearly all incorporated, fold in the cream.

7. Spoon into 4 small glass dishes, cover with cling film and refrigerate for an hour before eating.

8. Serve with a dollop of extra cream if your daily allowance permits.

*Nutritional Facts per serve: Calories 138, Fat 13.1g, Carbohydrate 4.4g, Dietary Fiber 0g, **Net Carbs 4.4g**, Protein 2.8g, **Calories from Fat 82%***

CHOCOLATE MACADAMIA ICE

Chocolate and nuts in a creamy iced base – enjoy.

Serves 6

INGREDIENTS:

1 cup (237ml) crème fraiche

1 cup (232g) full fat cream cheese

2 tbsp. unsweetened cocoa powder

2 tbsp. macadamia nut butter

1 tsp. xanthan gum

½ tsp. liquid stevia extract (adjust to taste)

1 ounce (28g) macadamia nuts, chopped (to sprinkle)

DIRECTIONS:

1. Place all of the ingredients except for the chopped nuts, in a food processor or blender and mix until everything is smooth and creamy.

2. Churn in an ice cream maker if you have one or place in a freezer proof container and place in the freezer.

3. If you are not churning the ice cream stir every 30 minutes as it is freezing to break up any ice crystals.

4. Freeze until required.

5. When ready to serve remove from the freezer about 10 minutes before serving to defrost a little.

6. Spoon into a serving dish and top with a tsp. chopped macadamia nuts for extra crunch.

Nutritional Facts per serve: Calories 296, Fat 29.5g, Carbohydrate 5.8g, Dietary Fiber 2.2g, **Net Carbs 3.6g***, Protein 5.4g,* **Calories from Fat 90%**

STRAWBERRY ICE CREAM

A creamy, fruity dessert to eat at any time of the day.

Serves 4

INGREDIENTS:

¾ cup (178ml) heavy cream

½ cup (116g) full fat cream cheese

1 tsp. strawberry extract

½ tbsp. xanthan gum

2 tsp. fresh lemon juice

½ tsp. liquid stevia extract (adjust to taste)

DIRECTIONS:

1. Place all of the ingredients in a large bowl and beat well together.

2. Churn in an ice cream maker if you have one or place in a freezer proof container and place in the freezer.

3. If you are not churning the ice cream stir every 30 minutes as it is freezing to break up any ice crystals.

4. Freeze until required.

5. When ready to serve remove from the freezer about 10 minutes before serving to defrost a little.

Nutritional Facts per serve: Calories 182, Fat 18.5g, Carbohydrate 3.4g, Dietary Fiber 1.6g, **Net Carbs 1.8g**, *Protein 2.8g,* **Calories from Fat 91%**

CHOCOLATE CHUNK ICE CREAM

This ice cream has a coco-nutty flavor with some lovely little sneaky chunks of chocolate hiding throughout.

Serves 8

INGREDIENTS:

2 cups (474ml) coconut cream

1 cup (237ml) heavy cream

½ tsp. liquid stevia extract (adjust to taste)

½ tsp. xanthan gum

1 tsp. vanilla extract

3 ounces (85g) dark chocolate (80% cocoa), chopped

DIRECTIONS:

1. Whisk together the coconut cream, cream, liquid sweetener and the gum.

2. Stir in the vanilla extract.

3. Churn in an ice cream maker if you have one or place in a freezer proof container and place in the freezer.

4. If you are not churning the ice cream stir every 30 minutes as it is freezing to break up any ice crystals.

5. Once half frozen stir in the chopped chocolate.

6. Freeze until required.

7. When ready to serve remove from the freezer about 10 minutes before serving to defrost a little.

Nutritional Facts per serve: Calories 293, Fat 29.1g, Carbohydrate 10.2g, Dietary Fiber 2.0g, **Net Carbs 8.2g**, *Protein 3.2g,* **Calories from Fat 86%**

MACA-MOCHA CREAM CRUNCH

A fluffy, chocolate flavored dessert with chopped toasted macadamias for crunch. This dessert will keep overnight in the refrigerator. Use rum essence instead of vanilla for a different taste.

Serves 2

INGREDIENTS:

¼ cup (59ml) sour cream

¼ cup (60ml) heavy cream

2 tbsp. unsweetened cocoa powder

1 tsp. strong brewed espresso coffee

½ tsp. vanilla extract

¼ cup (34g) macadamias, toasted and finely chopped

DIRECTIONS:

1. Beat together the creams until light and fluffy.

2. Beat in the cocoa powder, coffee and liquid sweetener together with the vanilla.

3. Fold through the toasted nuts and serve.

Nutritional Facts per serve: Calories 249, Fat 25.0g, Carbohydrate 7.0g, Dietary Fiber 3.2g, **Net Carbs 3.8g**, *Protein 3.6g,* **Calories from Fat 90%**

YOGURT CHEESECAKE

A no-bake creamy cheese cake, replete with zesty overtones of lemon.

Serves 12

INGREDIENTS:

4 tsp. unflavored sugar free gelatin

2 tbsp. cold water

¼ pint (118ml) hot water

2 cups (464g) full fat cream cheese

½ cup (118ml) sour cream

¾ cup (178ml) plain Greek yogurt (full cream)

3 medium eggs, separated

¼ tsp. liquid stevia extract (adjust to taste)

Pinch salt

1 tbsp. lemon juice, freshly squeezed

½ pint (237ml) heavy cream to decorate

DIRECTIONS:

1. Soak the gelatin in the cold water.

2. Add the hot water to the gelatin and stir to dissolve.

3. Beat together the cream cheese and the yogurt.

4. Add the lemon juice and beat again until fully incorporated.

5. In a small sauce pan, beat the egg yolks and sour cream and stir over a low heat until thickened.

6. Remove from the heat and add the gelatin mixture. Stir well.

7. Cool until it begins to thicken and then add to the yogurt cheese mixture.

8. Whisk the egg whites with the sugar substitute and when soft peaks form fold the whites carefully into the gelatin mixture.

9. Pour into a dish or individual molds and place in the refrigerator to set.

10. Leave for at least 4 hours before serving with a dollop of cream.

*Nutritional Facts per slice: Calories 264, Fat 25.4g, Carbohydrate 2.6g Dietary Fiber 0g, **Net Carbs 2.6g**, Protein 6.5g, **Calories from Fat 87%***

BLACKBERRY CREAM WHIZZ

Here's an instant iced smoothie with a few berries added for color and flavor. This does not keep particularly well so make it when you are ready to drink it.

Serves 2

INGREDIENTS:

¼ cup (36g) blackberries, frozen

½ cup (118ml) heavy cream

¼ cup (59ml) sour cream

¼ cup (59ml) coconut cream

6 drops liquid stevia extract (adjust to taste)

4 ice cubes

DIRECTIONS:

1. Place all of the ingredients in a blender.

2. Pulse to start and then blend until smooth.

3. Serve in a tall glasses.

Nutritional Facts per serve: Calories 265, Fat 26.8g, Carbohydrate 6.0g, Dietary Fiber 1.9g, **Net Carbs 4.1g**, *Protein 2.7g,* **Calories from Fat 91%**

VANILLA POPS

Ice cream on a stick! Sprinkle with a little grated dark chocolate or lemon zest, or use a different extract such as almond to experiment with changes in flavor. Add in a few drops of coloring for a fun look!

Makes 15

INGREDIENTS:

8 ounces (227g) full fat cream cheese

¼ cup (59ml) coconut cream

2 tbsp. coconut butter

4 ounces (113g) unsalted butter, softened

½ tsp. liquid stevia extract (adjust to taste)

2 tsp. vanilla extract

DIRECTIONS:

1. Beat together the cream cheese, coconut cream and the butters until light and fluffy.

2. Beat in the sugar substitute and the vanilla.

3. Line a cookie tray with parchment.

4. Place rounded tablespoonfuls of the mixture onto the parchment.

5. Use a teaspoon to form into rough little balls.

6. Insert a small lolly stick into each.

7. Place in the freezer and leave for at least an hour until hard.

8. Place in a suitable lidded container and store in the freezer.

9. Serve directly from the freezer.

*Nutritional Facts per pop: Calories 135, Fat 14.0g, Carbohydrate 1.3g, Dietary Fiber 0.5g, **Net Carbs 0.8g**, Protein 1.4g, **Calories from Fat 93%***

MASCARPONE LIME CREAMS

Enjoy these little zesty morsels as they are, or freeze for an icy treat.

Serves 8

INGREDIENTS:

1 cup (227g) mascarpone cheese

1 cup (237ml) heavy cream

¼ cup (59ml) coconut cream

1 tbsp. coconut butter

1 tsp. lime zest

2 tsp. lime juice, freshly squeezed

¼ tsp. liquid stevia extract (adjust to taste)

Pinch salt

DIRECTIONS:

1. Beat together all of the ingredients very well until you have a creamy consistency.

2. Spoon into 8 muffin cases and place in the refrigerator until ready to serve.

3. Freeze if not serving the same day.

Nutritional Facts per serve: Calories 142, Fat 13.2g, Carbohydrate 2.5g, Dietary Fiber 0.6g, **Net Carbs 1.9g***, Protein 4.2g,* **Calories from Fat 84%**

PEPPERMINT CHOCS

After dinner mint, anyone?

Makes 12

INGREDIENTS:

½ cup (116g) full fat cream cheese

¼ cup (23g) unsweetened shredded coconut

½ cup (113g) butter

1 tbsp. coconut butter

½ tsp. peppermint extract

Few drops green food coloring

3 tbsp. unsweetened cocoa powder

¼ tsp. liquid stevia extract (adjust to taste)

3 ounces (85g) dark chocolate (80% cocoa)

DIRECTIONS:

1. Beat together all of the ingredients except the chocolate.

2. Divide into 12 equal roundish portions – they can be rough - and place on a parchment lined cookie sheet.

3. Place in the refrigerator to harden for an hour.

4. Meanwhile melt the chocolate in a small ceramic basin over simmering water.

5. Remove from the heat and cool a little.

6. Drizzle the chocolate generously over the peppermint portions.

7. Leave to set before serving.

8. Keep in the refrigerator in an airtight container.

Nutritional Facts per choc: Calories 157, Fat 15.6g, Carbohydrate 5.0g, Dietary Fiber 0.8g, **Net Carbs 4.2g**, *Protein 1.9g,* **Calories from Fat 87%**

COCONUT CREAM MOUSSE

The whole family will enjoy this mousse so make a batch and watch them devour it. Keep in the refrigerator for a serving the next day.

Serves 8

INGREDIENTS:

1 cup (227g) mascarpone cheese

¾ cup (177ml) coconut cream

2 tbsp. coconut butter

1½ cups (355ml) heavy cream

2 fresh eggs, whites only

¼ cup (50g) powdered sugar substitute

DIRECTIONS:

1. Beat together the mascarpone and the coconut cream until smooth.

2. Beat in the coconut butter.

3. Beat the heavy cream in a separate bowl until soft peaks form.

4. Fold into the cheese mixture.

5. Beat the egg whites together with the sugar substitute until thick and dry.

6. Fold the whites into the coconut cream.

7. Pour or spoon into a serving bowl, cover with cling film and refrigerate for an hour to chill.

Nutritional Facts per serve: Calories 233, Fat 22.0g, Carbohydrate 5.5g, Dietary Fiber 1.4g, **Net Carbs 4.1g***, Protein 5.8g,* **Calories from Fat 85%**

BLUEBERRY FLUFF

Enjoy this quick and easy, near instant dessert for 2. Swap for raspberries to change up the flavor and lower the carb count a little more.

Serves 2

INGREDIENTS:

¼ cup (60ml) heavy cream

¼ cup (59ml) crème fraiche

2 tbsp. olive oil

¼ cup (37g) blueberries, frozen

6 drops liquid stevia extract (adjust to taste)

DIRECTIONS:

1. Place the crème fraiche, olive oil, blueberries and sweetener into a blender or small processor and pulse until smooth.

2. Scoop out of the blender and place in a medium sized bowl.

3. Whip the cream in a small bowl until soft peaks form.

4. Fold the cream into the blueberry mixture.

5. Serve in 2 small glass dishes.

*Nutritional Facts per fluff: Calories 244, Fat 25.6g, Carbohydrate 4.3g, Dietary Fiber 0.4g, **Net Carbs 3.9g**, Protein 2.7g, **Calories from Fat 92%***

MOCHA CREAM KICKSTARTER

Chocolate and coffee together give a heavenly mocha flavor. This creamy drink may be enjoyed hot or cold.

Makes 2

INGREDIENTS:

1 cup black coffee (as strong as you prefer)

½ cup (118ml) heavy cream

1 tbsp. coconut oil

1 tsp. vanilla extract

1 tbsp. unsweetened cocoa powder

Liquid stevia extract (adjust to taste)

1 tsp. powdered dark chocolate (80% cocoa), for dusting

DIRECTIONS:

1. Heat the coffee to just below boiling point.
2. Place the cocoa in a large mug.
3. Pour the hot coffee over the cocoa stirring well to allow the cocoa to dissolve.
4. Stir in the sweetener, vanilla essence and coconut oil.
5. Beat the cream until soft peaks form.
6. Stir half of the beaten cream into the warm coffee.
7. Top with the remaining cream and dust with the dark chocolate powder.
8. Drink hot or cold.

Nutritional Facts per serve: Calories 190, Fat 19.5g, Carbohydrate 3.8g, Dietary Fiber 0.9g, **Net Carbs 2.9g***, Protein 1.6g,* **Calories from Fat 92%**

HOT CINNAMON CHOCOLATE

Lovely on a cold winter's evening for that last snack before bedtime.

Makes 1

INGREDIENTS:

¼ cup (60ml) heavy cream

½ cup (119ml) hot water

2 tsp. olive oil

½ ounce (14g) dark chocolate (80% cocoa)

3 drops liquid stevia extract (adjust to taste)

½ tsp. vanilla extract

Powdered cinnamon to sprinkle

DIRECTIONS:

1. Place the water, cream, olive oil and chocolate in a small saucepan.
2. Heat gently together until the chocolate has melted and the liquid is just under boiling point.
3. Remove from the heat and stir in the vanilla and the sugar substitute – adjust to your taste.
4. Sprinkle on some cinnamon and stir.
5. Leave for a few moments for the flavors to develop before drinking.

*Nutritional Facts per serve: Calories 264, Fat 26.4g, Carbohydrate 7.8g, Dietary Fiber 0g, **Net Carbs 7.8g**, Protein 2.0g, **Calories from Fat 85%***

LEMON SMOOTHIE

A refreshing and cooling lemon smoothie.

Makes 1

INGREDIENTS:

¼ cup (60ml) heavy cream

¼ cup (59ml) crème fraiche

¼ cup (59ml) unsweetened almond milk

1 tsp. olive oil

1 tsp. fresh lemon zest

1 tsp. lemon extract

Few drops yellow food coloring

Liquid stevia extract (adjust to taste)

DIRECTIONS:

1. Place all of the ingredients in a jug and beat well together.
2. Pour into a glass and serve.

*Nutritional Facts per serve: Calories 287, Fat 28.5g, Carbohydrate 4.5g, Dietary Fiber 0g, **Net Carbs 4.5g**, Protein 2.7g, **Calories from fat 89%***

RASPBERRY CREAM

This sweet uses raspberries but you could easily substitute them for blackberries or a similar low calorie berry.

Serves 3

INGREDIENTS:

4 ounces (113g) full fat cream cheese

4 ounces (113g) heavy cream

2 ounces (57g) fresh raspberries

6 drops liquid stevia extract (adjust to taste)

DIRECTIONS:

1. Beat the cream cheese well until it is no longer lumpy.

2. Beat in the sugar sweetener.

3. Mash the raspberries and fold into the cream cheese.

4. Beat the cream until soft peaks form.

5. Gently fold into the cheese and raspberry mixture.

6. Spoon into 3 glass serving dishes.

7. Cover with cling film and refrigerate for an hour for the flavors to develop.

8. Serve topped with a little extra whipped cream if you have room for it in your calories.

Nutritional Facts per serve: Calories 272, Fat 27.3g, Carbohydrate 4.3g, Dietary Fiber 1.2g, **Net Carbs 3.1g**, *Protein 3.9g,* **Calories from Fat 90%**

CHOCOLATE CHEESE CUPS

These easy-to-make creamy little luscious morsels have a distinctive chocolate flavor. Top with extra cream and some grated dark chocolate if your daily count allows.

Makes 4

INGREDIENTS:

½ cup (118ml) heavy cream

½ cup (116g) full fat cream cheese

1 tbsp. unsweetened cocoa powder

½ tsp. salt

1 tsp. vanilla extract

¼ tsp. liquid stevia extract (adjust to taste)

DIRECTIONS:

1. Beat together all of the ingredients until well blended and smooth.

2. Spoon into 4 small serving cups.

3. Cover with cling film and refrigerate for an hour.

4. Serve and enjoy.

Nutritional Facts per serve: Calories 159, Fat 15.8g, Carbohydrate 2.0g, Dietary Fiber 0g, **Net Carbs 2.0g***, Protein 2.8g,* **Calories from Fat 89%**

COCONUT ORANGE FAT BOMBS

Keep a container of these in the freezer for an on-the-go snack. The piquant flavor of citrus gives these little morsels a lovely tang. They only have 100 calories each so allow yourself a couple for a serve.

Makes 18

INGREDIENTS:

½ cup (113g) coconut butter

½ cup (117ml) coconut oil

1½ tbsp. orange juice, freshly squeezed

2 tbsp. orange zest

½ tsp. liquid stevia extract (adjust to taste)

DIRECTIONS:

1. Line 18 mini muffin cups with liners or use a heat resistant silicone option such as an ice tray.

2. Place the coconut butter and coconut oil in a medium sized saucepan and gently heat them over a low heat.

3. When melted beat well to combine.

4. Beat in the sweetener, orange juice and zest.

5. Spoon equally among 18 mini muffin cases or into the individual compartments of an ice tray.

6. Place in the freezer to set.

7. When set store in the freezer in an airtight container.

Nutritional Facts per bomb: Calories 100, Fat 10.5g, Carbohydrate 2.0g, Dietary Fiber 1.3g, **Net Carbs 0.7g***, Protein 0.4g,* **Calories from Fat 95%**

CHOCOLATE MACADAMIA FAT BOMBS

Chocolate macadamia nut morsels to keep in the freezer. Each one has a pretty low calorie count, so you may just be able to sneak in a couple through your day!

Makes 36

INGREDIENTS:

1 cup (234ml) coconut oil

1 cup (240g) macadamia nut butter

4 ounces (113g) butter

2 tbsp. unsweetened cocoa powder

1 tsp. vanilla extract

½ tsp. liquid stevia extract (adjust to taste)

DIRECTIONS:

1. Place all of the ingredients except the sweetener into a medium sized saucepan.

2. Heat gently to melt the oil and the butters.

3. Add the sweetener and beat well together.

4. Pour into 36 heat resistant mini silicon molds or muffin cases. Some silicone ice-cube trays are perfect for this and have fun shapes.

5. Allow to cool and then place in the freezer to set.

6. Keep these in an airtight container in the refrigerator.

7. Enjoy!

Nutritional Facts per bomb: Calories 127, Fat 14.0g, Carbohydrate 1.3g, Dietary Fiber 0.8g, **Net Carbs 0.5g,** *Protein 0.8g,* **Calories from Fat 96%**

CREAMY NUT LAYER

A tempting dessert to help you enjoy your Fat Fast. This will keep for a night in the fridge and has around quarter of a Fat Fast daily calorie quota per serve.

Serves 2

INGREDIENTS:

2 ounces (57g) full fat cream cheese

¼ cup (36g) whole raw almonds, toasted

¼ cup (59ml) heavy cream

Liquid stevia extract (adjust to taste)

¼ tsp. pure vanilla extract

DIRECTIONS:

1. Place the nuts in a small blender and pulse until they are like coarse breadcrumbs.
2. Beat the cream cheese very well until it is smooth.
3. Beat in the cream until the mixture becomes light and fluffy.
4. Beat in a few drops of sweetener to taste, and the vanilla extract.
5. Place half of the nuts in the bottom of 2 small glass dishes.
6. Top with half of the cheese cream.
7. Add the rest of the nuts.
8. Top with the remaining cheese cream.
9. Cover with cling film and place in the refrigerator to chill.

Nutritional Facts per serve: Calories 255, Fat 24.4g, Carbohydrate 5.1g, Dietary Fiber 2.2g, **Net Carbs 2.9g**, *Protein 6.2g,* **Calories from Fat 86%**

This section contains lists to all of the recipes containing over 80% fat content in the Keto Living Cookbook range. With so many options, it's easy to stay on track during your Fat Fast!

As the recipes in the original series were not created with a Fat Fast in mind, make sure and remember to keep a close watch on the calorie count of each dish so as not to exceed your daily limits.

In most cases it's simple enough to adjust recipe quantities or portion sizes to make less or lower calorie servings if need be.

Keto Living Cookbook

Recipe	Fat %	Calories per serve
Cabbage and Chicken Soup	84%	338
Mushroom Soup with Fennel and Leeks	86%	586
Fresh Summer Soup	86%	266
Summer Avocado Soup	90%	266
Chilled Creamy Celery Soup	83%	279
Marinated Baby Tomatoes	92%	188
Cheese Snack Ball	83%	112
Vanilla Pudding	88%	156
Coffee Ice Cream	90%	180
Minty Chocolate Chip Ice	86%	185
Lemony Cheese Cake	86%	173

Refrigerator Cheesecake	87%	341
Strawberry Iced Cheesecake	84%	420
Chocolate Jelly	92%	288
Nutty Cheesecake Nibbles	87%	60
Coconut Chocolate Balls	82%	139
Creamy Coconut Candy	94%	341
Peanut Butter Cookies	87%	88
Pancakes Keto Style	83%	133
Almond and Goji Muffins	88%	137
Snickerdoodles	88%	97

Keto Living Cookbook 2

Recipe	Fat %	Calories per serve
Cheesy Sausage Balls	80%	189
Avocado Guacamole	83%	106
Cheddar Pancakes	80%	315
Seeded Crackers	80%	34
Cookies with Cream Cheese	89%	51

Peanut Butter Balls	84%	146
Mint Chocolate Fingers	81%	208
Lemon Meringue Swirls	80%	28
No Bake Choco Chews	83%	208
No Bake Nutty Cookies	86%	287
Fruity Fat Bombs!	98%	177
Chocolate Coconut Fat Bombs	92%	317
Lime Fat Bombs	99%	233
Tiramisu Treats	91%	323
Coconut Lemon Balls	86%	124
Choco Almond Truffles	81%	82
Creamy Chocolate Fudge	93%	104
Butterscotch Nut Squares	90%	263
Chocolate and Coconut Cupcakes	86%	427
Caramel Squares	90%	123
Chocolate Cheesecake	82%	330
Almond Cheesy Cupcakes	87%	211
Ginger Muffins	82%	201

Orange Cheesecake	84%	179
Iced Cinnamon Rolls	83%	281
Strawberry Ice Cream	88%	189
Chocolate Chip Pecan Bars	83%	247
Almond Cake	81%	258
Pecan Pie	87%	591
Carrot Loaf	83%	101
Little Heavenly Clouds	97%	133
Chocolate Cake	85%	167
Cream Custards	87%	275
Summertime Popsicle	89%	136
Hot Chocolate Nightcap	90%	254

Keto Living 3 – Color Cookbook

Recipe	Fat %	Calories per serve
Breakfast Cheesy Pancakes	89%	208
Intrepid Coffee	99%	223
Oopsie French Toasties	86%	579

Crunchy Cobb Salad	86%	524
Salmon and Avocado Boats	80%	371
Avocado and Tomato Cheese Salad	81%	554
Cream Cheese and Avocado Shake	85%	315
Pork Belly Slices	91%	651
Mushroom Soup	84%	330
Nutty Chocolate Cups	87%	186
Coconut Chocolate Squares	87%	214
Strawberry Cheesecake Nibbles	86%	229
Chocolate Cheesecake	86%	480
Chocolate Peppermint Mousse	87%	292
Chocolate Coconut Freeze	84%	313
Chocolate Nut Brownies	83%	391
Cinnamon Cream Cups	94%	281
Grandma's Egg Custard	87%	250
Keto Queen of Puddings	84%	301
Raspberry Chocolate Cheesecake	85%	598
Vanilla Cheesecake	83%	424

Chocolate Fluff Tartlets	89%	255
Nutty Cream Cheese Delights	83%	740
Orange Buns	80%	235
Red Velvet Cupcakes	82%	268
Lemon Butter Cakes	83%	302
Chocolate Blueberry Nut Muffins	83%	267
Nutty Ice Cream Layer	87%	412
Chocolate Chip Cookies	83%	161
Nutty Choco Bark	93%	173
Strawberry Smoothie	85%	339

THANK YOU

If you enjoyed these recipes, and I'm guessing your taste buds did, please keep an eye out for some of the other fun recipe books in the Keto Living Series!

Thanks so much to my family, my friends and the Keto community for keeping me loving all things Keto and making me smile every day.

Be good to each other!

Ella Coleman

THE KETO LIVING COOKBOOKS BY ELLA COLEMAN

Keto Living Cookbook: Lose Weight with 101 Delicious and Low Carb Ketogenic Recipes

The Keto Living Cookbook was written by Ella Coleman, an accomplished cook who loves experimenting with flavor combinations, and delights in eating and living a keto lifestyle.

It's no secret that carbs raise blood sugar, and our body produces insulin to get rid of it. The insulin then helps glucose convert to fat, and this is stored in our fat cells.

Goodbye self-esteem. Hello, cellulite!

On the ketogenic diet, carbs are limited and protein and fats are eaten in preference, keeping the body in a state of ketosis, and burning fats for a good, steady stream of energy.

The Keto Living Cookbook contains 101 recipes with easy-to-follow instructions for a scrumptious selection of meals and snacks straight from your kitchen to the table.

This book will be your constant kitchen companion with nutritional content, including a net carbohydrate, protein and fat count per serve listed for every single recipe. That's information you want, and need, right at your fingertips.

Lose the weight and love reaching your goals with the amazing selection of recipes to be discovered in the Keto Living Cookbook.

Keto Living Cookbook 2: Lose Weight with 101 Yummy & Low Carb Ketogenic Savory and Sweet Snacks

The Keto Living Cookbook 2 is a tasty new offering in the Keto Living series from accomplished cook, Ella Coleman.

Containing 101 delicious, easy-to-make sweet and savory snacks, this exciting new collection of recipes dispels the myth that a life without carbs means a life without fun foods or flavor.

How can we have our cake, and eat it too? Staying low carb, and in ketosis is the key.

With a little fun and creativity, combined with the right ingredients and instruction, you'll soon be making mouth-watering Ketogenic masterpieces that are a pleasure to the palate and perfectly suited to your goals.

From pizza to pancakes, muffins to meatballs, ice-cream and more, the recipes you'll discover in the Keto Living Cookbook 2 are designed to satisfy a hunger yet leave you feeling curiously guilt free in the blissful aftermath.

Nutritional info with a net carbohydrate, protein and fat count per serve has been calculated for every single recipe, along with easy-to-follow instructions, plenty of variety and includes a detailed introduction on which lowest carb ingredients best replace sugar in a Keto recipe.

Keto Living 3 – Color Cookbook: Lose Weight with 101 All New Delicious & Low Carb Ketogenic Recipes

Family meals... Mouthwatering snacks... Exquisite desserts...

Keto Living 3 - Color Cookbook is the latest outing of ketogenic creations by Keto cook Ella Coleman and is the most colorful to date, replete with beautiful photographs alongside every recipe.

The 1st Keto Living book took us on a journey through all of the courses; breakfasts, mains, and desserts.

The 2nd Keto Living book was a cornucopia of savory and sweet snack sensations, a delicious assault on the senses designed to debunk the myth that living Keto meant living boring.

The Keto Living 3 - Color Cookbook contains 101 all new delicious, low-carb and high fat recipes, and has been designed to showcase the amazing versatility & flavors a Ketogenic diet can offer.

Assisted in the kitchen by industry professional Nigel Burlington, Ella presents a perfectly balanced variety of both savory and sweet dishes for every course of the day, certain to satisfy all tastes and sure to keep you cooking wonderful Keto goodies for many moons to come.

And, as with all the Keto Living books, each recipe is replete with nutritional info and net carbohydrate count per serve, to help you stay informed and keep your journey on course. That's information you want, and need, right at your fingertips.

Lose the weight and love reaching your goals with the spectacular selection of beautifully depicted recipes to be discovered in the Keto Living 3 - Color Cookbook.

ADDITIONAL RECOMMENDED READING

If you already own all the recipe books in the Keto Living series, and are looking to expand your library, you may like to consider reading one of the excellent recipe books from blogger, Craig Clarke at www.ruled.me.

Craig is a valuable asset to the Keto community and I enjoy the effort and care he puts into his work. As is consistent with all of my books, Craig also provides nutritional breakdowns for every recipe. Being a carb counting data head myself, I find this essential!

Keto-fied!: Comfort Foods Made Low Carb

Your ketogenic diet doesn't have to be boring with this flavor-filled cookbook, packed with recipes that are creatively delicious and nutritious to boot. Keto-fied! skips the fluff and gets down to the nitty-gritty, serving up 43 classic low carb creations that are as easy to make as they are easy on the taste buds.

Keto-fied! contains inventive recipes that use seemingly unlikely ingredients to create mouth-watering dishes that you may have never thought you could eat again on a Keto diet.

REFERENCES

[1] Atkins, R. (1972). "Dr. Atkins' Diet Revolution" Robert Atkins, MD. New York: David McKay Inc.

[2] Reddit.com (/r/ketogains) [online] http://www.reddit.com/r/ketogains

[3] Reddit.com (/r/keto) [online] http://www.reddit.com/r/keto

[4] Banting, W. (1865). Letter on Corpulence: Addressed to the Public

[5] Kekwick A and Pawan GLS. Calorie intake relation to bodyweight changes in the obese. Lancet (1956) 155-161.

[6] Benoit FL, Martin RL, Watten RH. Changes in body composition during weight reduction in obesity. Ann Intern Med. 1965;63:604–12.

[7] Young CM, Scanlan SS, Im HS, Lutwak L. Effect of body composition and other parameters in obese young men of carbohydrate level of reduction diet. Am J Clin Nutr. 1971;24:290–296

[8] Volek JS, Sharman MJ, Love DM, et al. Body composition and hormonal responses to a carbohydrate-restricted diet. Metabolism 2002; 51:864–870.

[9] USDA Dietary Guidelines for Americans, 2010

[10] JS Volek, et al. Comparison of energy-restricted very low-carbohydrate and low-fat diets on weight loss and body composition in overweight men and women. Nutrition & Metabolism (London), 2004

[11] Qiao Y, Gao Z, Liu Y, et al. Breath Ketone Testing: A New Biomarker for Diagnosis and Therapeutic Monitoring of Diabetic Ketosis 2014; Biomed Res Int 2014.:869186

[12] Ketonix Acetone Breath Detector [online] http://www.ketonix.com

[13] Shai I, et al. Weight loss with a low-carbohydrate, Mediterranean, or low-fat diet. New England Journal of medicine, 2008; N Engl J Med 2008; 359:229-241

[14] Siri-Tarino PW, Sun Q, Hu FB, et al. Meta-analysis of prospective cohort studies evaluating the association of saturated fat with cardiovascular disease. The American journal of clinical nutrition 2010;91(3):535-46 doi: 10.3945/ajcn.2009.27725

[15] Chowdhury R, Warnakula S, Kunutsor S, et al. Association of Dietary, Circulating, and Supplement Fatty Acids With Coronary Risk: A Systematic Review and Meta-analysis. Annals of Internal Medicine. Published online March 18 2014

[16] Dashti HM, Al-Zaid NS, Mathew TC, Al-Mousawi M, Talib H, Asfar SK, et al. Long term effects of ketogenic diet in obese subjects with high cholesterol level. Mol Cell Biochem. 2006;286:1-9

[17] VanItallie, T., Nonas, C., Di Rocco, A., Boyar, K., Hyams, K., & Heymsfield, S. (2005). Treatment of Parkinson disease with diet-induced hyperketonemia: A feasibility study *Neurology, 64* (4), 728-730 DOI: 10.1212/01.WNL.0000152046.11390.45

[18] Krikorian R, Shidler MD, Dangelo K, et al. Dietary ketosis enhances memory in mild

cognitive impairment. Neurbiol Aging. 2012;33(2):425.e19-e27

[19] Friedman AN,Ogden LG et al. Comparative effects of low-carbohydrate high protein versus low fat diets on the kidney. Clin J Am Soc Nephrol 7;2012:p.1-9

[20] Renwick, A. et al. Sweet-taste receptors, low-energy sweeteners, glucose absorption and insulin release. British Journal of Nutrition advance online publication 10 July 2010; doi: 10.1017/S0007114510002540

[21] Ho KS, et al. Stopping or reducing dietary fiber intake reduces constipation and its associated symptoms. World J Gastroenterol 2012;18(33):4593-4596

[22] SodaStream [online] http://www.sodastream.com

Made in the USA
San Bernardino, CA
13 November 2014